ALAN SILLITOE

by Allen Richard Penner

Alan Sillitoe has established a reputation as an accomplished prose fictionist and as spokesman for the working-class point of view in contemporary England. He has received distinguished literary recognition for two of his works of fiction: the Authors' Club Prize for *Saturday Night and Sunday Morning* and the Hawthornden Prize for *The Loneliness of the Long-distance Runner.* Born of laboring-class parents in Nottingham, Sillitoe conveys in his works not only a keen awareness of the sensibilities of the poor, but an understanding of the general human condition in the twentieth century. This study provides a perceptive reading of Sillitoe's short stories, novels, and poems, relating them to the past and present literary tradition of England and Western Europe. It also presents an analysis of the New Left revolutionary spirit which pervades Sillitoe's works.

ABOUT THE AUTHOR

Professor Penner received his doctorate from the University of Colorado in 1965 and is an Associate Professor of English at the University of Tennessee where he teaches courses in the English, American, and European novel. A specialist in prose fiction, he has published articles in *American Literature, College Language Association Journal, Contemporary Literature, Renascence, Revue de Littérature Comparée, Southern Humanities Review, Studies in Short Fiction, University Review,* and *Xavier University Studies.* He is currently writing a book on depictions of madness and sanity in modern literature.

ALAN SILLITOE

by ALLEN RICHARD PENNER
University of Tennessee

Twayne Publishers, Inc. : : New York

FOR
MY MOTHER AND FATHER

PREFACE

Alan Sillitoe has an established reputation as an accomplished prose fictionist and as a spokesman for the proletarian viewpoint in England in the mid-twentieth century. He is the author of three collections of short stories, *The Loneliness of the Long-distance Runner* (1959), *The Ragman's Daughter* (1963), and *Guzman, Go Home* (1968); five novels, *Saturday Night and Sunday Morning* (1958), *The General* (1960), *Key to the Door* (1961), *The Death of William Posters* (1965), and *A Tree on Fire* (1967); three volumes of verse, *The Rats and Other Poems* (1960), *A Falling Out of Love and Other Poems* (1964), and *Love in the Environs of Voronezh* (1968); a travelogue, *Road to Volgograd* (1964); and several literary articles.

Two of his works have not only inspired successful cinema adaptations but have also merited distinguished literary recognition: Sillitoe received the 1958 Authors' Club Prize for *Saturday Night and Sunday Morning* and the Hawthornden Prize in 1959 for *The Loneliness of the Long-distance Runner*. Writing in the *New York Times Book Review* of April 10, 1960, Malcolm Bradbury said concerning *The Loneliness of the Long-distance Runner*, "Alan Sillitoe is certainly, on this showing, a major writer who ought to be read."[1] Of his *Saturday Night and Sunday Morning*, Anthony West observed in the *New Yorker* of September 5, 1959, "even if he never writes anything more, he has assured himself a place in the history of the English novel."[2]

Not all of his works have received such praise, nor should they have; but it is obvious that Sillitoe has already attained a position of consequence in contemporary English literature as a writer of prose fiction. It seems appropriate now—more than a decade after the publication of his first novel—that the several scholarly articles which have dealt with his works be supplemented by a more inclusive study devoted to all of the fiction and poetry which he has thus far produced.

The following study will first present a discussion of Sillitoe's life and his place in recent English literary history. Next follows an analysis of the three volumes of short stories and then of the five novels, which are discussed in the order of their publication. The final chapter assesses Sillitoe's accomplishments as a poet and his contribution to contemporary literature.

For permission to quote, I would like to acknowledge my appreciation to W. H. Allen for *The Rats and Other Poems* and *A Falling Out of Love and Other Poems;* to W. H. Allen and Alfred A. Knopf for *Saturday Night and Sunday Morning, The Loneliness of the Long-distance Runner, The General, Key to the Door, The Ragman's Daughter, Road to Volgograd,* and *The Death of William Posters;* to Macmillan and Company Ltd. and Doubleday for *A Tree on Fire, Guzman, Go Home,* and *Love in the Environs of Voronezh.* I would also like to thank the following editors for allowing me to publish preliminary studies of Sillitoe's works: Alexander P. Cappon for a study of *The Death of William Posters* and *A Tree on Fire* in *University Review;* L. S. Dembo, for a study of "The Loneliness of the Long-distance Runner" in *Wisconsin Studies in Contemporary Literature;* Frank L. Hoskins, Jr., for a study of "On Saturday Afternoon" in *Studies in Short Fiction;* and John Pick for a study of *Key to the Door* in *Renascence.*

I wish especially to thank Mr. Sillitoe for giving permission to quote from his works and for assisting me in preparing the biographical material in the book. I would like to express my appreciation to Miss Sylvia Bowman for giving me an opportunity to prepare this study and to the Graduate School of the University of Tennessee for the financial assistance which has made it possible for me to complete the book. Lastly, I would like to express my appreciation to my wife, for her kind encouragement and consideration.

Allen Richard Penner

University of Tennessee
August, 1970

CONTENTS

CHRONOLOGY

1928   Alan Sillitoe born March 4, in Nottingham, England, the second of five children of Sylvina and Christopher Sillitoe, a tannery laborer.

1933   Attended public schools in Nottingham.

1942–   Left school to work at the Raleigh Bicycle Company and
1946   subsequently at A. B. Toone (a plywood manufacturer) and at B. Firman Engineering. Employed as an airfield controller at Langar Airfield, Nottingham.

1947–   Served as a radio operator with the Royal Air Force in Malaya.
1948   While hospitalized for a year with tuberculosis, composed several hundred poems, a few short stories, and the first draft of a novel, all of which he destroyed.

1949–   Lived and wrote in Nottingham and in southeast France, inland
1952   from Menton.

1953–   Worked as a translator and English teacher in Majorca and
1958   composed *Saturday Night and Sunday Morning,* "The Rats," and most of the stories in *The Loneliness of the Long-distance Runner.*

1957   *Without Beer or Bread* (poems republished in *The Rats and Other Poems*).

1958   *Saturday Night and Sunday Morning,* awarded the Authors' Club Prize for the best English first novel of the year. Published in the United States in 1959.

1959   November 19, married Ruth Esther Fainlight, a New Yorker by birth and a poet.

1959   *The Loneliness of the Long-distance Runner* awarded the Hawthornden Prize. Published in the United States in 1960.

1960   *The General;* appeared in the United States in 1961.

1960   *The Rats and Other Poems.*

1961   *Key to the Door;* United States edition, 1962.

1963   *The Ragman's Daughter;* appeared in the United States in 1964.

1964   *A Falling Out of Love and Other Poems.*

1964   *Road to Volgograd;*   United States edition the same year.

1965   *The Death of William Posters;* appeared in the United States the same year.

1967   *A Tree on Fire;* published in the United States in 1968.

1968   *Guzman, Go Home;* United States edition, 1969.

1968   *Love in the Environs of Voronezh;* United States edition, 1969.

CHAPTER 1

Life and Works

ALAN SILLITOE was born on March 4, 1928, in Nottingham, the second of five children of Sylvina and Christopher Sillitoe, a tannery laborer. Both the time and social circumstance of his birth are of major importance to Sillitoe's later development as a writer. His works have been called a historical curiosity, a throwback to the proletarian literature of the 1930's.[1] Thematically, some of them are such curiosities, for they contain the political attitudes and revolutionary sentiments of an older generation of English radicals even though they are set in the 1950's and 1960's. One of his works, *Key to the Door,* is simply historical rather than a historical curiosity, however, for it represents the period of Sillitoe's childhood in Nottingham in the 1930's. Written over a period of twelve years, this novel is, according to Sillitoe, the most autobiographical of his works.[2] With other documents, it provides some suggestion as to the nature of the author's early life.

I *The Lessons of Nottingham*

Sillitoe was born shortly before the great economic depression, when England, like most of the rest of the Western world, was reduced to a subsistence economy. In 1929, the unemployed in Great Britain numbered approximately 1,000,000; early in 1931, the figure had risen to 2,600,000, and by September, at the height of the crisis, it stood at 2,900,000. Not until July, 1935, did the figure fall below 2,000,000.[3] Existence for a family like the Sillitoes, supported by the dole and by the occasional wages of a semiskilled laborer, was extremely difficult. In *Key to the Door,* Sillitoe vividly depicts the frustrations of a similar family, the Seatons. Harold, the father, unable to read and incapable of finding steady employment, resorts to the dole to support his family. Finding that means of subsistence inadequate to feed his wife and children, he turns to theft, which earns him a two-month sentence, and the compensation of state support of his family while he is in prison. When he is released, the cycle of poverty continues. The family exists by living in one slum dwelling after another, making its moves in the dead of night to avoid rent collectors. The family's circumstance is one of continual struggle against the economic conditions which threaten its existence.

The experience of living in poverty has left an indelible imprint upon Sillitoe's mind and upon his art. There are few of his stories, poems, and novels which are not concerned with those people who exist in the lower reaches of society. His clear understanding of the circumstances and the psychology of poverty is evidenced in various paragraphs from an essay which he has written on the subject:

Your world becomes small, intense and real. Your senses are sharpened but, strangely enough, this doesn't necessarily mean an increase in intelligence, or the ability to act. Intelligence is often stunted in the fight for order and food. A near-cretin, mustering energy in order to survive, may present a dextrous visage to the better-off, who imagine he must be cunning to survive at all on so little.

The very poor are too busy surviving to want to get on. To get on is something often dinned into them, handed down by the culture beneath which they exist. They are unable to take advantage of it, for to reach next week with clothes on your back, food still on the table, and enough life in your brain to face another week is the most they can do.

. . . .

There are degrees of being poor. The most common is that of the man who earns twelve pounds a week and has a couple of children. If he is living in London he may pay four pounds a week for a room, and his wife will be unable to go to work because the children can't be left alone. This is not usually regarded as poverty. In such a room you might find a telly or radio. The man will smoke cigarettes, go to the pictures now and again, drink a pint maybe—all in small degree, after his rations are secure, sometimes when they are not.

. . . .

If a poor family doesn't throw some of its money away each week on fags and the pictures they may go under quicker than if they do. Their morale cracks, and they end up either in the poor-house or the looney bin. This is a reason for the so-called fecklessness of the poor: a visit to the pictures is often better than a hot dinner.

. . . .

The worst poverty of all is that which afflicts the man who is out of work for a long time, through no fault of his own. This is a destitution of the spirit as well as a destitution of material means—the man who wants work yet has to see his children never quite getting enough to eat, who knows that something should be done about his situation but is powerless to do anything on his own. Such a man becomes filled with bitterness.

The poor know of only two classes in society. Their sociology is much simplified. There are *them* and *us*. Them are those who tell you what to do, who drive a car, use a different accent, are buying a house in another district, deal in cheques and not money, pay your wages, collect rent and telly dues, stop for you now and again at pedestrian crossings, can't look you in the eye, read the news on wireless or television, hand you the dole or national assistance money; the shopkeeper, copper, schoolteacher, doctor, health visitor, the man wearing the white dog-collar. Them are those who robbed you of your innocence, live on your backs, buy the house from over your head, eat you up or tread you down.[4]

This essay, which is revealing in several respects, evidences not only that Sillitoe knows how the poor feel but that he continues to feel from their point of view. One seldom suspects, in reading of the characters whom he creates, that the author is a man on the outside looking in. Rather, he seems to be so much a part of what he creates that it never occurs to him that he could look upon the poor from any point of view other than that of an insider. This personal involvement differentiates his writing from that of an author like D. H. Lawrence, whose origins, like Sillitoe's, were in the poor laboring class of Nottingham, but, even in the most autobiographical of his novels, *Sons and Lovers,* Lawrence—as narrator—leaves the distinct impression that he has removed himself from the life which he describes. It is as though he had—through learning, through achievements—risen above a past that in retrospect is seen to have been sordid and regrettable, however poignantly he may render the tragedy of the hero, Paul Morel. Morel, like the author, looks with disdain upon the common people with whom he is forced to associate. Asked to go to the coal-mine office to collect his father's wages, Paul objects to the vulgarity of the people whom he will deal with there: "They're hateful, and common, and hateful, they are, and I'm not going any more. Mr. Braithwaite drops his "h's', an' Mr. Winterbottom says 'you was.' "[5] Lawrence is so sympathetically and emotionally involved with the problems of Paul

Morel that his artistic objectivity sometimes suffers; but he is not similarly involved with the people who share his social origins.

Brian Seaton, the hero of Sillitoe's most autobiographical novel, never feels himself separated from those of his social class; and neither, we feel, does the author. The probable nature of Sillitoe's youth is suggested in the story of Brian, who is reared amid violent family quarrels engendered by both his father's moody nature and by the frustrations of poverty. He is well schooled in the "fang and claw" existence of the Nottingham slums. His playgrounds consist of the comparatively idyllic rural residence of his grandparents, as well as a sprawling Nottingham trash dump. He inherits the anger of his father, but he possesses a sensitive intelligence which enables him to rise above, but not forget, his origins. His natural interest in reading brings him into conflict with his parents.

In detailing this conflict, Sillitoe effectively conveys the difficulties involved in a youth of the Nottingham slums becoming, as he has become, a man of letters. To Brian's parents, who in the past have had difficulty enough surviving, spending money on books is inevitably associated with frivolous waste. Even in more plenteous times, after the depression years, money spent on books was money that could have been spent for food or clothing; within the context of poverty, the acquisition of knowledge is morally wrong, unless it can be attained without cost. A scene from the novel illustrates the circumstance. At the age of ten, Brian, having purchased *The Count of Monte Cristo* with pennies carefully saved, is rebuked by his parents:

"Yer've wasted 'alf a crown on a book?" his father exclaimed. He'd imagined they'd be pleased with his cleverness in bringing such a thing into the house, but it was the opposite. It was as though he'd been split in half and was bleeding to death. All for a book. "It was my money," he cried, anguished and bitter, because instead of buying the book he should have given the money to them.

"You're bloody-well silly about books," his father said, a definite threat in his voice. "You read till you're bloody-well daft." His mother came back from the kitchen: "You stand need to spend half a crown on books when you ain't got a bit o' shoe to your feet. And you're a sly little swine to 'ave money in the 'ouse all that time when I've often bin wi'out a shillin' ter buy some snap." (168)

While the public schools might have resolved the difficulty of obtaining an education, these institutions, as Sillitoe depicts them, simply impede rather than aid the educative process. After ending his formal schooling at the age of fourteen, Sillitoe took a job in the Raleigh Bicycle Factory, where his father was also employed. Between 1942 and 1946, he worked there and at two other firms, the A. B. Toone Company (a plywood manufacturer) and at B. Firman Engineering. The details of Brian Seaton's employment at a firm called Robinson's Cardboard Factory and Arthur Seaton's work as a lathe operator in a bicycle factory (in *Saturday Night and Sunday Morning*) suggest the nature of Sillitoe's experiences. Brian finds the work given him both difficult and dangerous. The manager of the factory allows him to work extra hours, in violation of the Factory Act regulating the working conditions of youths under sixteen. The duty which Brian performs, cleaning soot from a stoke-hole flue, has both immediate and long-range hazards. Breathing the hot, dust-laden air of the furnace could lead to unconsciousness and suffocation, or it could contribute to future respiratory ailments, such as the tuberculous condition which Sillitoe later developed.

While Brian's work is hazardous, Arthur Seaton's is simply monotonous. As the operator of a capstan lathe, he is responsible for producing each day hundreds of identical parts, a task of mind-deadening dullness. On the basis of his own experience, Sillitoe re-creates vividly the smells of the factory—oil-suds, metal shavings, lubricants—the sights and noises of the factory: conveyor belts creaking and rumbling, laden with hubs, nuts, bolts; the grinding of lathes, the stamp of punch presses. He catalogues as well the state of mind produced by the factory environment: "You began the day by cutting and drilling steel cylinders with care, but gradually your actions became automatic and you forgot all about the machine and the quick working of your arms and hands and the fact that you were cutting and boring and rough-threading to within limits of five-thousandths of an inch" (35). The labor, performed in a state of semiconsciousness, has the effect, if carried on throughout a lifetime, of disabling the mind for any intellectual stimulation more demanding than that conveyed by the television tube. From this, Sillitoe determined to escape.

II *The Developing Writer*

After ending his factory employment, Sillitoe worked as a controller at Langar Airfield in Nottingham and served from 1947 to 1948 with the Royal Air Force in Malaya, as did Brian Seaton in *Key to the Door*. There their stories diverge. The novel ends with Seaton preparing to return to England to flex his "laboring muscles" to open the door to the future. Sillitoe, hospitalized for almost a year while in Malaya, used the forced rest to begin his career as a writer. He wrote several hundred poems, some short stories, and the first draft of a novel, all of which he destroyed.[6] After receiving his discharge from the service and a pension of forty-five shillings per week, he continued to write, living for a time in Nottingham; in Soler, France; and, from 1953 to 1958, in Majorca. There he and his wife, the former Ruth Esther Fainlight, lived, supplementing Sillitoe's pension by his efforts at translating and teaching and by her work as a travel-agency courier. During this time, Sillitoe sent several of his poems to Robert Graves, who was also living in Majorca at Deya. At Graves's invitation, Sillitoe visited him one Sunday, riding a borrowed bicycle to Deya, where Graves had built a home in the 1930's from the royalities of *I Claudius.* Their meeting was informal and cordial. Graves finished autographing a limited edition of poems while they talked of England and the problems which writers face. Sillitoe records portions of their conversation:

"some of your poems are good," he said, still looking at me as if waiting for some sort of recognition. "At least you end them well. So many people get off to a good start, then fizzle out half way through, coming in lamely at the end." . . . I said I found his remarks about my poetry encouraging, but that so far none had been published. "That doesn't matter," he replied. "As long as you keep on writing them." This wasn't the sort of truth I wanted to hear: "I'd still like to see them in print."

"That is no problem if you keep writing." [7]

Sillitoe, who continued to write in Majorca, produced the manuscripts for his first novel, *Saturday Night and Sunday Morning;* his first long poem, *"The Rats";* and six excellent tales which appeared in his first collection of stories: "Mr. Raynor the School-Teacher," "The Fishing-Boat Picture," "Noah's Ark," "On Saturday Afternoon," "The Disgrace of Jim Scarfedale," and "The Decline and Fall of Frankie Buller."

However, like most writers, Sillitoe found success a beguiling but elusive siren. After nine years of writing, he had managed to get into print only one small collection of poems, *Without Beer or Bread* (1957). When he returned to England in 1958, *Saturday Night and Sunday Morning* was in the process of being rejected by three publishing houses. In that same year, however, Sillitoe's professional fortunes began to turn. W. H. Allen elected to publish *Saturday Night and Sunday Morning,* which received the Authors' Club Prize for the best English first novel of 1958. In the following year, *The Loneliness of the Long-distance Runner* appeared and was awarded the Hawthornden Prize for Literature. The release of cinema versions based upon these two works enhanced Sillitoe's reputation and, of course, increased the sale of his books.

Having established himself as a promising young author, Sillitoe began to publish works at a steady pace. Between 1960 and 1967 he released for publication two volumes of verse, another collection of short stories, a travelogue, and three novels. Some of these had been in the process of composition long before the period which saw their publication. *The Rats and Other Poems* (1960) contains pieces written between 1950 and 1960; the title poem, which Sillitoe considers to be his most important poetic work, was composed in Majorca in 1956 and 1957. *The General* (1960), an allegorical novel presenting a global conflict between two forces called "East" and "West" was originally conceived, like *Saturday Night and Sunday Morning,* as a short story that was first written in 1949 in Nottingham shortly after Sillitoe returned from his tour of duty with the Royal Air force in Malaya. By the time he was living in Majorca, in 1953, it had taken the form of a novel; seven years later, after several revisions, it appeared in its final form.

Key to the Door (1961), perhaps because it is largely autobiographical, was longer in composition than any of the author's other novels. The section depicting the protagonist's military service in Malaya was composed during 1949, following Sillitoe's return from that country. The childhood section, which contains some of the author's best writing, was first written during 1950. Sillitoe has said of the composition of the work: *"Key to the Door* was in fact an amalgamation of two early novels, very much rewritten, with a third section (Ropewalk) added. . . . They were consistently re-written and altered however up to the date of publication in 1961." [8] Thus, the criticism of some reviewers that Sillitoe was rushing works into print is not wholly appropriate.

The Ragman's Daughter (1963), the second collection of short stories, was written between 1959 and 1962 at Hertfordshire, Notting Hill Gate; it is composed of seven stories previously published in *The New Yorker, The Guardian, Argosy, The London Magazine, New Statesman, Transatlantic Review,* and *The Daily Worker.* The travelogue, *Road to Volgograd* (1964), grew out of a month-long trip sponsored by the Writers' Union. It is a warm, sympathetic, and quite biased appraisal to the Soviet government and people. In contrast to his attitude toward his own country, Sillitoe finds everything to praise and little to blame in Russia. The second volume of poems, *A Falling Out of Love* (1964), was composed between 1960 and 1964 in various places. The themes, like those of Sillitoe's earlier poems, center upon violence, *angst,* revolution, and love. His *The Death of William Posters* (1965), a novel written in London, Tangier, and in Deya, Majorca, between August, 1962, and November, 1964, carries to even greater lengths the social, religious, and political rebellion which characterize his earlier fiction. The same may be said of *A Tree on Fire* (1967), composed in London and Majorca between April, 1964, and April, 1965. The novel is a sequel to *The Death of William Posters* and is the second volume of a projected trilogy. His latest publication—*Guzman, Go Home,* a collection of short stories, and *Love in the Environs of Voronezh,* a volume of poetry—both appeared in 1968.

III   *Sillitoe and the "Angry" Tradition*

When *Saturday Night and Sunday Morning* appeared in 1958, it seemed to reviewers and critics that Sillitoe had written a type of proletarian *Lucky Jim* (1954), despite the occasional anarchistic grumblings of the novel's hero, Arthur Seaton. Accordingly, Sillitoe was grouped with other novelists who were at the time being labeled "angry young men": Kingsley Amis, John Wain, and John Braine. Sillitoe facetiously acknowledged the association himself in *The Death of William Posters* by referring to an imaginary novel, *"Hurry on Jim* by Kingsley Wain that started by someone with eighteen pints and fifteen whiskies in him falling downstairs on his way to the top" (166), which is, in effect, a description of Arthur Seaton's entrance in *Saturday Night and Sunday Morning.*

Grouping Sillitoe with those novelists is less appropriate now than in 1958 or 1959, and it was not wholly appropriate then. John Wain's Charles Lumley of *Hurry on Down* (1953) is indeed angry, but his anger is not of the same quality or intensity as that of Sillitoe's heroes. Lumley most resents the boorish nature of "the respectable," those who "wear a uniform" of purposefulness. His aim is not to reform but to escape the values and the class system of society by remaining aloof, and he at last attains what he calls "neutrality" by working as an anonymous gag writer for a radio comedian. The job gives him the economic security which he desires, but makes him, ironically, a part of the educated middle class which he had attempted to escape, but to which he belongs.

Jim Dixon of Amis' *Lucky Jim* is, of course, less an angry young man than a humorous, bumbling, befuddled young man. His rebellion against the pretensions of *academia,* like Charles Lumley's rebellion against middle-class values, ends in an adjustment to society and in a partial acceptance of its values. Dixon wins a beautiful girl and a better job, a fanciful conclusion appropriate to the humorous tone of the novel. But Sillitoe's works have more often been compared with those of John Braine, partly because their heroes seem to have a kindred anger, and partly because both authors are from working-class backgrounds. Braine's *Room at the Top* (1957)—which Sillitoe may have reference to in his description of a character "falling downstairs on his way to the top"—demonstrates, however, the important differences between them. While Sillitoe's heroes champion the poor and despise the rich, Braine's Joe Lampton desires most of all to imitate the rich, culturally and materialistically, and he refers with disdain to the laboring class, into which he has been born, as "the overalled and sweaty,"[9] an attitude clearly alien to Sillitoe and his heroes.

A work from the same general period but more closely in accord with Sillitoe's spirit is John Osborne's drama, *Look Back in Anger,* which seemed to Sillitoe, when he first saw it performed in the spring of 1957, to be the harbinger of a new era in British letters: "Jimmy Porter's shrapnel bombs were bursting with marvellous accuracy above the neatly stacked sandbags of Coward and Rattigan. I knew that the front was wide open, and to me it was a more impressive and spectacular breakthrough than *Lucky Jim* had been on the fiction sector a few years earlier."[10] Sillitoe's enthusiasm is clearly genuine, but the bellicose images he selects to convey his praise suggest why, in the final analysis, *Look Back in Anger* would not seem to him the most significant dramatic achievement of the day. Jimmy Porter's anger expresses a sense of urgency, of justifiable rancor, and of needed redress; but one realizes, finally, that his anger is essentially egocentric and directionless, as, for example, when Porter reflects, "I suppose people of our generation aren't able to die for good causes any longer. We had all that done for us, in the thirties and the forties, when we were still kids."[11] For Sillitoe, the social causes worth fighting and dying for are legion, despite the general increase in Britain's prosperity during the past twenty years.

It is not surprising, in retrospect, that the work which Sillitoe found to be closest in spirit to his own was written not by Kingsley Amis,

John Wain, John Braine, or even by John Osborne, but by John Arden, whose *Serjeant Musgrave's Dance*[12] espoused the same violent social rebellion which has gradually come to dominate Sillitoe's poetry and prose. Arden's play, in its details of costume and setting, suggests England of the period 1860-90, although the exact time of the setting is not given. The message of the play, however (as its subtitle—*An Unhistorical Parable*—suggests), is intended to bear relevance as much to the present as to the past. Its theme, in part, is that violent overthrow of the government, the rich, the clergy—the Establishment in general—is both justified and desirable as a means of correcting current social evils and redressing the wrongs of the past. Sillitoe clarifies his attitude toward the place of revolution in social reform in his sympathetic reaction to Arden's rebellious hero, Black Jack Musgrave: "The rage of Black Jack was a step beyond the anger of Jimmy Porter—both were melancholics, and Arden took Black Jack as far as one can go in this direction—to extreme yet understandable rebellion so that where Jimmy ended married, Musgrave hanged."[13]

This early appreciative response to "extreme yet understandable rebellion" suggests that Sillitoe was never, really, simply an "angry young man." His hostility was not a transitory emotion of youth but a conviction well grounded in his identification with the working class and with revolutionary causes. As the following chapters indicate, this sense of identity permeates Sillitoe's works.

CHAPTER 2

The Loneliness of the Long-distance Runner

THE NINE stories in *The Loneliness of the Long-distance Runner,* which were written during a period of eight years, from 1950 to 1958, represent some of the best short fiction that Sillitoe has written. There is a certain vitality and freshness in them that seems to have diminished somewhat in Sillitoe's later fiction. The dominant themes in these stories are the alienation of the individual in society, the *angst* of modern civilization, and the struggle of man to attain personal identity in what seems to be an increasingly impersonal world. It is not unusual for a contemporary prose fictionist to take these subjects as the center of his concern—they have virtually dominated modern literature.

It is unusual, however, to find an author who is capable of revitalizing these care-worn subjects with the skill which Sillitoe brings to his first collection of short stories. What distinguishes his writing in this instance is that he does not simply submit that there are, indeed, many things about which one might reasonably and justifiably despair, and then happily roll about in the thought with ill-concealed pleasure. Rather, he brings to the task the hard-earned talents that his craft demands: a knowledge of his people, an understanding of the dramatic tension attainable in the short-story form, and a fine sense of what constitutes the human situation.

This chapter considers seven of the nine stories in *The Loneliness of the Long-distance Runner.* First to be treated are three tales—"On Saturday Afternoon," "Noah's Ark," and "The Disgrace of Jim Scarfedale"—which present a subject that Sillitoe always handles remarkably well: the educative experiences of boys who have grown up, as Sillitoe did, in the laboring-class districts of Nottingham. Two stories which deal with marital difficulties, "The Match" and "The Fishing-boat Picture," are excellent examples of the psychological tension which can be created in the short story. The last part of the chapter is devoted to Sillitoe's novelette "The Loneliness of the Long-distance

Runner," generally considered to be the best English short novel of the decade in which it appeared; finally, there is a brief discussion of the story which Sillitoe uses as a type of epilogue in which the author speaks directly to the reader, "The Decline and Fall of Frankie Buller."

I   *"On Saturday Afternoon," or, "What Are Yo' Looking So Bleddy Black For?"*

Professor Dennis Hurrell, while praising Sillitoe's verisimilitude, has observed justly that he "has taken his material from the working-class life without relating it, except peripherally, to the viewpoints of any other social group, and has projected it through the eyes of the members of that class." [1] While Sillitoe has taken the "have-nots" as his primary subject, he usually avoids the error of presenting them as a homogeneous group, acting out their half of a timeless dichotomy in a pantomimed struggle against those ancient antagonists, the "haves." If Sillitoe's talents extended no further than that, we might well expect his works to take a place in due time alongside such nineteenth-century triumphs of social dualism as Charles Kingsley's *Alton Locke* (1850), Mrs. Gaskell's *North and South* (1855), or Charles Reade's *Put Yourself in His Place* (1870).

In fact, although Sillitoe inevitably regards the representatives of the "system" with the Cyclopean eye of a polemicist rather than with the three-dimensional vision required of an author, he does not, in his more successful works, accord such treatment to the primary subject of his fiction, the laboring class, which becomes, at times, the thieving class. These he endows with a diversity of humanity that moves them beyond the narrow confines of "class." Needless to say, this quality is not uniformly indigenous to his or to any other author's works, but it is particularly evident in "On Saturday Afternoon." The story is set in a factory town similar to Sillitoe's native Nottingham and is narrated by a sixteen-year-old boy who recalls how, at the age of ten, he had watched a man attempt to commit suicide by hanging himself from a light fixture.

The dominant theme of the story—one that recurs throughout Sillitoe's works—concerns what the author calls a "bleddy blackness," a quality which at first seems to be the psychological equivalent of "nada" in Ernest Hemingway's "A Clean, Well-Lighted Place," perhaps the most famous treatment of the theme in modern short fiction. [2] While there is no evidence of influence, there are, in fact, several significant parallels and contrasts between that story and "On Saturday

Afternoon." In Hemingway's tale, as in Sillitoe's, there is a character (the elderly habitué of the café) who seeks to escape the "nada" through an abortive suicidal hanging; in addition, each story deals with characters who seem insensible to the whole matter of despair, and each focuses upon a central character who, while conscious of the problem, chooses to endure it rather than resort to suicide. In the presentation of the central characters the stories differ significantly, however. For Hemingway's elder bartender, "it all was nada y pues nada y nada y pues nada. Our nada who art in nada." Moreover, the future held for him only sleepless nights and empty days that, apparently, he was to · bear passively, even stoically: "He would lie in the bed and finally, with daylight, he would go to sleep. After all, he said to himself, it is probably only insomnia. Many must have it." The case is otherwise for the protagonist of "On Saturday Afternoon."

The youthful narrator of Sillitoe's story, who might reasonably be described as a twentieth-century embodiment of the candor, but not the innocence, of Huckleberry Finn, introduces in the opening paragraph two important elements: the difference between illusion and reality, and the matter of "blackness":

I once saw a bloke try to kill himself. I'll never forget the day because I was sitting in the house one Saturday afternoon, feeling black and fed-up because everybody in the family had gone to the pictures, except me who'd for some reason been left out of it. 'Course, I didn't know then that I would soon see something you can never see in the same way on the pictures, a real bloke stringing himself up. I was only a kid at the time, so you can imagine how much I enjoyed it. (118)

If we are struck by the blunt announcement that a suicidal hanging is in the offing, we are equally struck by the off-hand tone that our narrator has assumed to relate the affair. Such enthusiasm for seeing "a real bloke stringing himself up" may seem to be senselessly callous; but, as we shall see, the attitude bears an important relation to what the author has to say about the impersonality of modern society and about those who look upon reality and those who do not.

Following the introduction, the young man abandons the matter of suicide and digresses to tell us about his family. Initially, it seems that Sillitoe has made an expedient concession of structure in order to add to the credibility of his youthful narrator, who, aged sixteen, and only semiliterate, might be expected to tell a rambling, rather than an economically coherent, tale. The digression, however, is apparent rather than real, for the suicide episode, although it is the central dramatic action of the story, is not an end in itself. Instead, it is one of several manifestations of despair that constitute the broader subject of the tale.

What we learn from the narrator's digression is that "blackness" is a characteristic of his whole family; the nature of the condition is illustrated in a description of the father: "I once saw him broodier than I'd ever seen him, so that I thought he'd gone crackers in a quiet sort of way—until a fly flew to within a yard of him. Then his hand shot out, got it, and slung it crippled into the roaring fire. After that he cheered up a bit and mashed some tea" (119). How a man becomes "black" is not stated explicitly—for there may well be no patent explanation—but answers are suggested throughout the story.

Such a condition seems to arise in part from the anonymity of modern urban, industrial society, where the most rudimentary form of personal identification, the proper name, is not common currency. The lack of individual identity within the community is suggested in the story by such seemingly incidental comments as the narrator's, "But outside the air wasn't so fresh, what with that bloody great bike factory bashing away at the yard-end. I didn't know where to go, so I walked up the yard a bit and sat down near somebody's back gate" (120). Extracted from context, the statement seems too trivial to merit notice; but, if we reflect, what has been expressed is not at all the same as saying, "I sat down near Smith's back gate," or even "I sat down near a back gate," which emphasizes the impersonality of an inanimate object rather than the impersonality of its owner. "Somebody" is utterly anonymous, just, as we note, are all of the characters in the story, who are given appellations no more individualized than "the bloke," "mate," "the copper," and, pointedly, "old what's-his-name."

In Sillitoe's world, loneliness is not an experience peculiar to long-distance runners. Still another factor seems to bear an important relation to "blackness." The laboring-class people whom the author depicts—if they do not operate outside of the law as do the protagonists of "The Loneliness of the Long-distance Runner," "The Ragman's Daughter," and "The Good Women," to mention only three instances—engage in work that is either physically exhausting or mentally monotonous, or both. We are not told the specific occupation of the narrator's father, but a picture of the man at his leisure leaves little doubt concerning the nature of his toil: "He just sits, almost on top of the fire, his oil-stained Sunday-joint maulers opened out in front of him and facing inwards to each other, his thick shoulders scrunched forward, and his dark brown eyes staring into the fire. Now and again he'd say a dirty word, for no reason at all, the worst word you can think of, and when he starts saying this you know it's time to clear out" (118).

It is not enough simply to observe that the labor that has thickened the shoulders has thickened the mind and spirit as well and to let the matter drop at that. For, as Sillitoe manages to recognize in this, if not in all of his stories, "blackness," and the difficulty of living in general are not experiences peculiar to any one social class. As Sillitoe has himself observed, "Some people think realism is synonymous with 'working-class,' whereas realism means showing people as individuals as well as the values they live by."[3] Ultimately, the factors that differentiate one individual from another, or one family from another, in their ability to endure the human predicament may be so elusive as to defy explanation. Hemingway's elder bartender explained the difference between himself and his helper—who had no comprehension of the significance of the "nada"—by saying, "It is not only a question of youth and confidence although those things are very beautiful," but, "We are of two different kinds." Correspondingly, Sillitoe's narrator rejects his first, simple explanation of his father's black looks—"All because of a packet of fags"—and concedes that "Mostly, I suppose there's nothing to look so black for: though it's nobody's fault and you can't blame anyone for looking black because I'm sure it's summat in the blood" (119).

Those who, like Hemingway's young bartender, do not have such blood, are of an entirely different breed. As Sillitoe's youth observes, "Some people get fed-up and don't look bad at all: they seem happy in a funny sort of way, as if they've just been set free from clink after being in there for something they didn't do, or come out of the pictures after sitting plugged for eight hours at a bad film, or just missed a bus they ran half a mile for and seen it was the wrong one just after they'd stopped running" (119). The implication is that these happy souls are not burdened by the travail of serious reflection. Sillitoe conveys the predicament of those who cannot avail themselves of such bliss when he has his narrator add, "but I can never get any sort of answer even if I sit and think for hours, which I must admit I don't do, though it looks good when I say I do. But I sit and think for long enough, until mam says to me, at seeing me scrunched up over the fire like dad: 'What are yo' looking so black for?' " (119). The answer is, quite simply, that he has looked at the world and reflected seriously upon what he has seen.

Two modes of response to the lot that is man's have thus far been presented: those who simply do not think about it; and those who, thinking about it, scrunch over the fire, say a dirty word "for no reason at all," and, when things get dreary enough, cheer themselves up by turning over "a table full of pots and all." The third alternative is, of course, suicide. Fittingly, Sillitoe endows the suicide with an ectomorphic physiognomy that suggests a thought-laden man: "He was tall and thin and had a face like a parson except that he wore a flat cap and had a moustache that drooped and looked as though he hadn't had a square meal for a year" (120). Entering the stage, he is greeted not by anonymous indifference, but by its half-sister, petulant curiosity:

> ... I remember that as he turned in by the yard-end one of the nosy gossiping women who stood there every minute of the day except when she trudged to the pawn-shop with her husband's bike or best suit, shouted to him: "What's that rope for, mate?"

> He called back: "It's to 'ang messen wi', missis," and she cackled at his bloody good joke so loud and long you'd think she never heard such a good'un. . . . (120)

Following his welcome by this descendant of Shakespeare's weird sisters, he is joined by the narrator, who follows him, as he explains, "having nothing better to do because I hadn't gone to the pictures" (121). When the two are inside the man's house, Sillitoe develops the tension superbly, heightening the horror through the quizzical petulance of the boy, who observes helpfully twice that the light cord probably will not support a full-grown swinging man (it did not), and through the calm purposefulness of the young man, who whistles a "fancy tune" to himself as he knots the rope and explains, " 'I'm going ter 'ang messen, lad' ... as though he'd done it a time or two already, and people had usually asked him questions like this beforehand" (121). The narrator then asks the man the inevitable question of why, and he replies with deceptively simple efficiency, "Because I'm fed-up. ... And because I want to. My missus left me, and I'm out o' work" (122).

The reply is reasonable enough; but as an explanation of the act of suicide, it is not much more helpful than the narrator's accounting for the "blackness" of his father with, "All because of a packet of fags." Another job might be obtained, and with luck, another missus, or at least the old one retrieved—if the character possessed a certain spirit to survive and, as William Faulkner expressed it, "to endure." The answer carries with it a significant point: no circumstantial condition will go very far in explaining why a man acts as he does. Since Sillitoe does not choose to explain suicide with some solution similar to his earlier, "I'm sure it's summat in the blood," he has his narrator turn to the next logical alternative, the man's physiognomy. He is surprised to note, as perhaps is the reader, that for one about to attempt suicide, "He wasn't looking black at all, nowhere near as black as anybody in our family when they're feeling fed-up" (121). Then the narrator renders the distinction precisely: "Also there was a funny look in his face: even when he talked to me I swear he couldn't see me. It was different to the black looks my old man puts on, and I suppose that's why my old man would never hang himself, worse luck, because he never gets a look into his clock like this bloke had. My old man's look stares at you, so that you have to back down and fly out of the house: this bloke's look looked *through* you, so that you could face it and know it wouldn't do you any harm" (123).

In this description, the narrator puts into place the third and final element of the theme of illusion versus reality: if, at one end of the scale, there are those who reject the burden of reality simply by not thinking about it, who "seem happy in a funny sort of way, as if they've just . . . come out of the pictures after sitting plugged for eight hours at a bad film," at the other end are those who avoid the burden by looking through reality, who abdicate the first, instinctive responsibility of man and beast alike, to survive and endure. It is precisely this instinct that Sillitoe applauds in this story, as well as in his most widely read works, "The Loneliness of the Long-distance Runner" and *Saturday Night and Sunday Morning.*

Following his presentation of the unsuccessful suicide attempt, the author introduces a policeman, who is caricatured as a representative of the callousness of the "system," through such remarks as "It ain't your life. And it's a crime to take your own life. It's killing yourself. It's suicide" (126). Evidently as inept as unfeeling, the police make the error of incarcerating the suicide on the sixth floor of the hospital, from which he promptly jumps, succeeding in his endeavor at last. Indicating once again that the suicide itself is part of a broader theme in the story, Sillitoe does not portray the death scene directly, but he has the narrator report the facts of the case as he has obtained them from a woman who worked at the hospital "dishing grub out and tidying up." After Sillitoe outlines the details of the suicide, the story returns to the narrator, who provides something of a final summation of the theme. Reflecting on the whole matter of despair, the boy concludes:

The black coal-bag locked inside you, and the black looks it puts on your face, doesn't mean you're going to string yourself up . . . because when you're feeling that black you can't even move from your chair. Anyhow, I know I'll never get so black as to hang myself, because hanging don't look very nice to me, and never will, the more I remember old what's-his-name swinging from the light-fitting.

More than anything else, I'm glad now I didn't go to the pictures that Saturday afternoon when I was feeling black and ready to do myself in. Because you know, I shan't ever kill myself. Trust me. I'll stay alive half-barmy till I'm a hundred and five, and then go out screaming blue murder because I want to stay where I am. (126-27)

The narrator's promise at the beginning of the story that he had seen "something you can never see in the same way on the pictures," refers at last not only to the attempted suicide but also to the nature of reality and of life itself. The blackness that is "summat in the blood" of the young man and his family is no less than a concomitant of their ability to look at the world and think about it—and to survive the experience, which, Sillitoe suggests, is no mean feat. The youth will not avoid reality by immersing himself in the illusory world of "the pictures"; nor will he, like the suicide, slide away from life gradually until he only looks "through" it. The boy's assertion that "hanging don't look very nice to me, and never will," is not the same as the desparing "nada" of Hemingway's weary bartender and of the literature of the "Lost Generation" generally. The boy's outlook reveals a spirit that can look candidly upon the gross and sometimes cruel reality that is life and yet survive the task and even endure. This same quality typifies young Colin and Bert of Sillitoe's "Noah's Ark" and their adult counterparts, the concupiscent Arthur Seaton of *Saturday Night and Sunday Morning* and the swift-footed Smith of "The Loneliness of the Long-distance Runner."

II *"Noah's Ark"*

In "Noah's Ark," a story remarkably similar in themes and tone to "On Saturday Afternoon," Sillitoe presents one significant episode in the education of a Nottingham youth who comes to recognize the difference between the fustian cloth of reality and the gaudy but unwearable tinsel of illusion. The tale opens in a school classroom, where those who have come with the hope of finding reality must sometimes satisfy themselves with its opposite. The subject of the school lesson is, as the author tells us, "a book of dream adventures"—a series of "meanderings" which are unraveled by a teacher in a droning, deadening voice. The title of the schoolbook, *Masterman Ready,* suggests a genre to which Sillitoe's own works are unalterably opposed on esthetic, if not on moral, grounds: the ancient and unending literature of romance, with its superhuman, unconquerable heroes.

Upon such romantic literature Colin, the young subject of Sillitoe's tale, has been nurtured. If *Masterman Ready* has failed to render truthfully the reality of the world, it has performed the traditional function of romance—escape: "The sum total of such free-lance wandering took him through bad days of scarcity, became a mechanical gaudily dressed pied piper always ahead, which he would follow and one day scrag to see what made it tick. . . . With imagination fed by books to bursting point, he gave little thought to the rags he wore . . ." (100). The sound which jars Colin from the illusory world of *Masterman Ready* comes, suitably, from without rather than from within the classroom, it comes from the passing of drays and trucks loaded with the components of a Noah's Ark Carrousel, Dodgem Cars, Ghost Trains, and other attractions of the annual Goose Fair, an event which presents yet another type of irresistible illusion which Sillitoe described in *Saturday Night and Sunday Morning:* "noise and lights a magnetized swamp sucking people into it for miles around" (170).

To this event Colin goes with his cousin Bert, who, at age eleven, is a year older and considerably wiser than Colin in the ways of the world. The events and the dialogue that occur while they are walking to the fair serve to illustrate the difference between them: Bert who has in the past robbed candy shops at midnight, realizes, with pride, that Colin does not have the nerve to do such a thing. More importantly, Bert has come to recognize that moral perfection is impossible and that occasional minor failings are not worth bothering his conscience about. Sillitoe makes the point in connection with the least escapable of all realities—poverty. Colin, thinking of his four-penny wealth as he walked along with Bert, "was glad of its power to take him on roundabouts, but the thought of what fourpence would do to the table at home filled him—when neither spoke—with spasms of deep misery. Fourpence would buy a loaf of bread or a bottle of milk or some stewing meat or a pot of jam or a pound of sugar. It would perhaps stop the agony his mother might be in from seeing his father black and brooding by the hearth if he—Colin—had handed the fourpence in for ten Woodbines from the corner shop" (101-2).

With the economic circumstance of the protagonists defined in such precise terms, the financial question becomes a moral one, as it frequently does in Sillitoe's works. Colin further reflects, "It was marvellous what fourpence would do, if you were good enough to place it where it rightly belonged—which I'm not, he thought, because fourpence would also buy a fistful of comics, or two bars of chocolate or take you twice to the flea-pit picture-house or give you four rides on Goose Fair, and the division, the wide dark soil-smelling trench that parted good from bad was filled with wounds of unhappiness" (102).

The moral question presented looms, side by side throughout the story, with the matter of illusion versus reality. The "bad" represented here obviously is so only in terms of a ten-year-old's manner of thinking. The comics, chocolate, pictures, and carnival rides that Colin desires will be displaced in due time by the pleasures of liquor, tobacco, women, and fishing which fill the leisure moments of Arthur Seaton, the hero of *Saturday Night and Sunday Morning.* Both sets of pleasures have one thing in common—they are momentary diversions from reality: in Colin's case, from rags, hunger, and family quarrels; in Seaton's case, from the monotonous and mindless work in which he is engaged from Monday morning until Friday night. The same type of work and the same adult diversions more than likely will fill Colin's later years. The clue to the whole matter, as Bert knows, and as Colin will recognize, is that unhappiness arising over pangs of conscience at such "badness" is suspect. In Sillitoe's works, evil is made of sterner stuff; it centers more often than not upon the callousness that consistent avarice engenders in man.

Sillitoe's heroes are cunning in the matter of survival, but their cunning seldom inflicts any lasting harm upon others; and it never becomes jaded avarice. In Bert's case, for example, survival is a marginal achievement: he is "ever-sharp and hollow-cheeked with the fire of keeping himself going, lit by an instinct never to starve yet always looking as if he were starving" (102). Nor does the struggle for survival kill human sympathy in Sillitoe's characters, indeed, a strong bond of companionship exists between Bert and Colin, and a feeling of loyalty resides in each boy for his immediate family. While Bert will not take four pence home—recognizing that such a sum is better spent enjoyably and quickly forgotten, for all the good it would do—he would give his mother part of "five bob or a pound" that he might come into. While he does not bother to take found cigarettes to his father, he does bother, as he searches through packets cast down along the street, to slip "picture cards" in his pocket for his younger brothers. Such affection, however, seldom crosses family lines or even less frequently, social-class lines; for the world in which Sillitoe's characters move is usually typified by financial exploitation and by a failure of human consideration.

Since the author either ignores or denies the validity of religious considerations, morality is defined in terms of man's actions in society. Precisely what that consists of is indicated in the boys' first encounter with humanity inside of the fairgrounds: "A tall gipsy-looking woman with black hair done up in a ponytail stood in the penny-a-roll stall, queen of its inner circle. She stared emptily before her, though Colin, edging close, sensed how little she missed of movement round about. A stack of coppers crashed regularly from one hand to the other, making a noise which, though not loud, drew attention to the stall . . ." (104). The "inner circle" of which the lady is queen is not limited to the penny-a-roll stall at Goose Fair. The empty stare, the acute perception of threatening movement, and the deft shifting of coins are all to be found in an impersonal society, or jungle, in which the boys move, where most considerations are subordinate to acquisitiveness.

Bert, who has already gone far in learning how to survive in such an environment, does not hesitate to steal some coppers from the man who is rolling pennies at the stall. Caught in the act, he is clever enough to turn the accusation upon the victim by lying, "Them's my pennies. . . . It's yo' as is the thief, not me. You're a bully as well. . . . I worked 'ard for that, at our dad's garden, diggin' taters up and weedin' " (105-6). Throughout the whole argument, the "queen of the inner-circle" looks "vacantly—sending a column of pennies from one palm to another—beyond them into packed masses swirling and pushing around her flimsy island" (106). She expresses the impenetrable indifference that characterizes the real jungle, where questions of right and wrong are ultimately resolved through strength or cunning. Ultimately, the robbed man relents and gives Bert the pennies, which the boys spend at various pleasures within the next hour.

Before beginning the most important dramatic incident in the story, the "Noah's Ark" scene, Sillitoe suggests vaguely the story of Eve and the serpent, as it might be transformed in the tawdry and mercantile environment in which his characters move: Bert becomes "paralysed at the sight of a half-dressed woman in African costume standing beside a paybox with a python curled around her buxom top." When Colin remarks, "it's a wonder that snake don't bite her, ain't it?" Bert replies with cryptic humor: "It's the sort that squeezes yer ter death, but they gi' 'em pills to mek 'em dozy" (106-7). Sillitoe's fictional world is devoid of innocence, and it holds no promise of heaven. It is a place where the Big Wheel spins "its passengers towards the clouds, only to spin them down again . . ." (108). Colin, unable to distinguish between illusion and reality, is deceived by the gaudy spectacles of the fair; and he believes that they comprise "a heaven-on-earth because together they made up the one slender bridgehead of another world that breached the tall thickets surrounding his own" (109). The illusion is one which is quickly dispelled.

The story moves to the central allegory as Bert and Colin, once again penniless, approach the irresistibly enticing Noah's Ark. In the biblical account of the Flood, all men but Noah and his family were excluded from the ark because "God saw that wickedness of man was great in the earth, and that every imagination of the thoughts of his heart was only evil continually" (Gen. 6:5). Although Sillitoe's characters lack "innocence," nowhere in his work does he accept the notion of man as naturally sinful. Rather, in the jungle world which his characters inhabit, passage on the ark turns upon the possession or the lack of a few pennies. Bert, skilled in the ways of survival, suggests to his cousin that cunning is always as negotiable a currency as pence, and then he proves it by climbing aboard the ark and skillfully circling just behind the paymaster (a grotesque distortion of Noah) as the whole mass of human beings and wooden animals moves on the "flying circular up-and-down world rolling round at full speed" (107).

When Bert returns safely from his stolen ride, the challenge devolves on his cousin, who is still attempting to reconcile his notions of morality with the rules of survival which regulate the "jungle." Sillitoe indicates the path of his reasoning: "Colin well knew that it was wrong, and dangerous, which was more to the point, yet when a Noah's Ark stood in your path spinning with the battle honours of its more than human speed-power written on the face of each brief-glimpsed wooden animal, you had by any means to get yourself on to that platform, money or no money, fear or no fear, and stay there through its violent bucking until it stopped" (110).

The attraction which the ark holds for Colin lies, in part, in the fascination of its danger; but it also offers, like the literature of romance, illusory promises: "Watching from the outside it seemed that one ride on the glorious Noah's Ark would fill you with similar inexhaustible energy for another year, that at the end of the ride you wouldn't want to come off, would need to stay on for ever until you were either sick or dead with hunger" (110). Once on the ark, however, Colin finds that watching from the "inside" is altogether another experience.

In the revolving maze of wooden animals and human limbs, Colin stumbles awkwardly against the paying passengers as he attempts to keep a safe distance behind the money collector; he encounters "enraged astonished faces" and vindictive, "irate fists" pummeling him for the disturbance he is causing. Sillitoe makes the point explicit; the "Noah's Ark" has in effect become a reflection of reality: "This jungle was little different from home and street life, yet alarming, more frightening because the speed was exaggerated" (112). The author develops the chaotic experience with superb verisimilitude as Colin pursues his dizzying course from tiger to zebra to crocodile. Abruptly, the money collector, "an overalled greasy bastard whose lips clung to a doused-out nub-end, cashbag heavy but feet sure"—a vindictive Noah "controlled by a wink from the centre" (112-13)—turns upon the stowaway.

In that instant, Colin conceives the deadly and important difference between illusion and reality with a clarity impossible in the classroom: "The soporific, agreeable summer afternoons of *Masterman Ready,* having laid a trap at the back of his mind, caught him for a moment, yet flew away unreal before this real jungle in which he had somehow stumbled" (111). Retracing his steps on Noah's Ark in a desperate and vain attempt to escape retribution, Colin finally conceives the moral point of the human situation in a different light: "No rest for the wicked, his mother always said. But I'm not wicked, he told himself. You'll still get no rest though. I don't want any rest. Not much you don't" (112). The theme recurs throughout Sillitoe's novels and short stories: man finds himself in a situation of bad luck and travail not of his own making, and he must somehow find the cunning and spirit to endure.

When the money collector catches Colin, he grabs him by the "neck-scruff and waist," whereupon the boy kicks wildly, gains his freedom, and hurls himself from the spinning Ark, "crashing like a sensitive flesh-and-bone cannonball between a courting couple and piling against the wooden barrier" (114). The lessons of reality are hard ones, but the point of the story is not simply pessimistic; instead, it is, as we have indicated, that man must survive the blows of fate and emerge unbroken in spirit. Colin does both, with the aid of cousin-companion Bert, who provides the human consideration not usually available in the jungle world: "Bert bent down and came up with him on his shoulders like an expert gymnast, going white in the face and tottering down the wooden steps, towards warm soil and dust. On the last step he lost his strength, swerved helplessly to the right, and both donkey and burden crashed out of sight by the bottom roundabout boards where no one went" (115).

After that Cervantic rendering of courageous, hapless human

fellowship, the story ends with the two passing from view, arm-in-arm in the fog-bound streets, singing a child's parody of "Rule Britannia" at the top of their voices: "Rule two tanners/ Two tanners make a bob, / King George nevernevernever/ SHAVES HIS NOB!" The nonsensical irreverence of their song evidences just the sort of spirited, fustian vainglory that can survive and endure the human predicament. If Colin has been tossed from Noah's exclusive Ark along with most of the rest of mankind, he has not drowned in the callous sea of humanity which surrounds him. Sillitoe's portrayal of this spirited will to survive, even more than his presentation of class conflict, characterizes his writing at its best.

III   *"The Disgrace of Jim Scarfedale"*

"The Disgrace of Jim Scarfedale" is a tour de force that is largely sustained by the personality of the narrator. The reader is struck by his colorful dialectal language, by his swaggering egoism, and by his spirited acceptance of the proposition that every human endeavor will inevitably be undone by bad luck or by the folly of man, but that man must nevertheless struggle and play the game to the end. The tale begins,

I'm easily led and swung, my mind like a weather-vane when somebody wants to change it for me, but there's one sure rule I'll stick to for good, and I don't mind driving a nail head-first into a bloody long rigmarole of a story to tell you what I mean.

Jim Scarfedale.

I'll never let anybody try and tell me that you don't have to sling your hook as soon as you get to the age of fifteen. You ought to be able to do it earlier, only it's against the law, like everything else in this poxetten land of hope and glory. (139)

Jim Scarfedale is a young man who has remained with his domineering mother so long that he does not know "the difference between an apron string and a pair of garters," a fate which the narrator is determined to avoid—if necessary, by a dramatic escape: "bike to Derby, bus to Manchester, train to Glasgow, nicked car to Edinburgh, and hitch-hiking down to London" (140). The plan of the escape is romantic, as is the notion that the serious problems which confront man can be escaped by geographic relocation; but the narrator anticipates the reader's objection: "Yes, I know, every city's the same when you come to weigh it up: the same hostels full of thieves all out to snatch your last bob if you give them half the chance; the same factories full of work, if you're lucky; the same mildewed backyards and houses full of silverfish and black-clocks when you suddenly switch on the light at night; but nevertheless, even though they're all the same they're different as well in dozens of ways, and nobody can deny it" (140). If man is recalcitrantly dishonest, if he must always expect the same humdrum work, the same bug-infested environment, there is still hope, which resides as always in the outlook he chooses to take, in seeing in the whole circumstance an endless diversity. Monotony is as much a state of mind as it is a state of existence. The subject of this story is a particular mind which is incapable of overriding the obstacles which are part of its existence.

Jim Scarfedale lives near a bicycle factory, a phenomenon which with its noisy engines, pulleys, and metal presses may, as the narrator suggests, have contributed as much to Jim's condition as his mother has. But his mother, "a big woman, a Tartar, a real six-footer who kept her house as clean as a new pin, and who fed Jim up to his eyeballs" (140), is the dominating force of the story. She is motivated by that particular kind of matriarchal possessiveness which is something other than love. Her husband has died of consumption, and she is the sole ruler of the home and of Jim. When she learns that her son has, without her knowledge, made arrangements to be married, she is infuriated. The narrator's retelling of her reaction turns paraphrase into parody:

His mam hadn't even seen the girl, and that was what made it worse, she shouted. Courting on the sly like that and suddenly upping and saying he was getting married. . . . Ungrateful, after all she'd done for him, bringing him up so well. . . . Think of all the times she'd slaved for him! Think of it! Just think of it!. . . . Day in and day out she'd worked her fingers to the bone at that fag-packing machine, coming home at night dead to the world yet cooking his dinners and mending his britches. . . . And now what had he gone and done, by way of thanks? (Robbed her purse? I asked myself quickly in the breathless interval; pawned the sheets and got drunk on the dough, drowned the cat, cut her window plants down with a pair of scissors?) No, he'd come home and told her he was getting married, just like that. (141-42)

To this tirade, which is sustained for two pages, Jim responds not at all (not having the opportunity to); and the mother at last exacts a promise from him that he will bring his betrothed to their home for a visit—for an inspection. The girl, Phyllis, does not prove to be what the narrator and the neighborhood expect, "some poor crumby-faced boss-eyed tart from Basford" (144). Rather, she has finesse, and she can even respond gracefully to the mother's greeting, "I hear as you're wanting to marry my lad?" (145), and to the suggestion that she is pregnant. There is danger in the finesse, however. Scarfedale has escaped from a mother who is one of the tribe of "domineering strugglers" only to become prey to a woman who has married a man of the laboring class because of her sociological theories. Jim discovers that "she had some idea that a working bloke like myself was good and honest and all that sort of thing. . . . She used to say that it was a treat to be able to marry and live with a bloke like me who used his bare hands for a living . . . at night she used to talk about politics and books and things, saying how the world was made for blokes like me and that we should run the world and not leave it to a lot of money grabbing capitalist bastards . . ." (149). When the novelty diminishes and she discovers that Jim Scarfedale is a rather lackluster individual, not the "noble savage" she imagined, she makes life difficult: she gives him only cigarettes and toffee for dinner, sets his newspaper afire, hurls the poker at him, sits nude in the living room, and at last runs away to London with the "four pounds ten and three pence" from the jam jar.

Scarfedale returns to his mother a broken man, takes to frightening little girls at midnight, and is at last arrested and jailed for his acts. The conclusion of Jim Scarfedale's story is tragi-comedy, but the narrator's epilogue points up the moral: if those of the working class (or of any class, for that matter) are to survive, they must have the spirit to assert their own independence, to cut themselves free of apronstrings of whatever nature—the past in particular—and to avoid the clutches of such uplifters as Phyllis, who soon weary of the moral pleasure of saving the downtrodden masses.

The narrator, maintaining to the end his independence, reasserts his intention to break away, "up through Derbyshire and into Manchester, then up to Glasgow, across to Edinburgh, and down again to London, saying hello to mam and dad on the way" (155). Serving as a foil to the weak-willed Jim Scarfedale, the narrator points up the themes of "On Saturday Afternoon" and "Noah's Ark"—that the world is a difficult testing ground which requires courage and fortitude of those who wish to survive.

IV *"The Match"*

Sillitoe's tales of youth are complemented by his stories of adults among the working class. "The Match" centers upon a character type frequently found in Sillitoe—the man who, for reasons which are not entirely clear, is so disgusted with life that he makes himself and his family miserable. The story opens on a cold, rainy evening at a football match where Lennox, an aging automobile mechanic, is a spectator. Possessed with a "one-track pessimism," he feels instinctively that the home team will lose because "he himself, a spectator, hadn't been feeling in top form" (128). When the shoulders of the spectators in front block his view, he thinks with anger that they "had swayed in front purposely to stop him seeing" (129). His sight, which has been failing during recent years, at times can only perceive "a mass of grey squares dancing before his open lids" (128); and he remembers, after the game has ended in defeat for the home team, that the preceding day he had gotten into a fight because a fellow worker had called him "Cock-eye."

In contrast to the abject spirit of Lennox is the youthful vigor of Fred Iremonger, who shrugs off the defeat of the team with thoughts of returning to the warmth of his home and the sexual embrace of his young wife, which, he reasons, will be even more pleasurable for the contrast that it will make to the disappointment of the football match. Lennox's only comment on Fred's happiness in marriage is "all that'll alter in a bit" (131), which prepares the reader for the scene which follows.

As soon as Lennox returns home, he begins baiting members of his family for an argument: "He walked through the small living-room without speaking, took off his mac in the parlour. 'You should mek a fire in there,' he said, coming out. 'It smells musty. No wonder the clo'es go to pieces inside six months" (135). His wife is sitting in the living room knitting; she has prepared the dinner and set the table; the three children are just finishing tea. Lennox commands the eldest child, a girl of fourteen, to make a fire in the parlor; when she expresses a desire to finish her tea first, Lennox forces her to do his bidding by offering to strike her. The dinner, consisting of kippers, is unsatisfactory; Lennox carefully separates the bones from the flesh, making two piles in his plate. He feeds the flesh to the cat; then, "when he considered that it had eaten enough he kicked it away with such force that its head knocked against the sideboard" (136). He demands that one of his sons be sent to buy pastries and that his wife make fresh tea. When his wife objects to both orders, he picks up the plate of fish and "with exaggerated deliberation" throws it on the floor. This precipitates a crisis in which Mrs. Lennox shouts "You're a lunatic . . .

you're mental," and she ultimately takes the children and leaves her husband "for the last time."

The condition of Lennox, like that of "Dad" of "On Saturday Afternoon," is a type of self-destroying and family-destroying blackness for which no clear explanation is given. It cannot be explained in terms of economic circumstances, for there is food on the table—food to be thrown away, in fact. What we sense throughout is that Lennox becomes a "lunatic" out of monotony—the monotony of his work, his marriage, his mind. His reaction to the food which his wife serves him is symptomatic of a larger problem in his existence: "One of these days . . . we'll have a change" (136). The hope, in the terms of the story, is an empty one, for Sillitoe seems to suggest in such presentations that men become caught in a trap of drudgery, marriage, and aging, from which there is no escape. The final comment of the story is an ironic one, spoken by the wife of the young Fred Iremonger, whose apartment adjoins that of Lennox. Overhearing the row that has taken place next door, she slips off her husband's knee, straightening her skirt, and observes of Lennox's anger, "Just because Notts have lost again. I'm glad yo' aren't like that" (137).

V   "The Fishing-boat Picture"

Among Sillitoe's works of short fiction, "The Fishing-boat Pictures" is an exceptionally successful story, and its success depends in no small degree upon two factors: first, it is not a polemical discussion of the sociological problems surrounding the struggle between "haves" and "have-nots"; second, as in all of his more successful works, Sillitoe gives the impression of having completely subordinated his own personality to that of his characters. The story is narrated by a fifty-two-year-old Nottingham postman, Harry, who recounts the major events of his married life and attempts to grasp their significance. The narrator is literate but not "learned": "If I started using long and complicated words that I'd searched for in the dictionary I'd use them too many times, the same ones over and over again, with only a few sentences—if that—between each one; so I'd rather not make what I'm going to write look foolish by using dictionary words" (79). The narrator's purpose is to discover the meaning of his past. Of his having been a postman for twenty-eight years, he concludes, "such a fact has no significance whatever," while the experience of being married for twenty-eight years "is very important no matter how you write it or in what way you look at it" (79).

Being married is "very important," but Sillitoe seems to parody the way in which human beings, more like marionettes than anything else, accept unquestioningly the progressive stages of life: education, job, marriage, old age, death. Harry recalls that, as soon as he had obtained his position at the post office, Kathy, his future wife, had said, " 'you know what we're to do now you've got a steady job, son't you?' 'Get Married,' he replied. 'And that was that. She gave me the best kiss I'd ever had, and then we went into the wood' " (80).

If "the wood" bears a figurative as well as a literal sense, the *double-entendre* is appropriate; for, as the narrator explains, "the bare fact of my getting married meant only that I changed one house and one mother for another house and a different mother. . . . The trouble was that when we had a row—and there were rows, swearing, hurling pots: the lot—it was too much like suffering, and in the middle of them it seemed to me as if we'd done nothing but row and suffer like this from the moment we set eyes on each other, with not a moment's break, and that it would go on like this for as long as we stayed together" (81). It seems that Sillitoe is simply presenting a vignette of human misfortune: the misery in marriage of two persons whose natures unsuit them for each other's constant company. But the author probes beyond the external symptoms of the misalliance to the fundamental cause of the problem.

The spat which precipitates Kathy's leaving home occurs following dinner, "plates empty and bellies full so that there was no excuse for what followed." When the argument begins, Harry is engrossed in a book as his wife says,

"I do love you Harry. . . . Harry, look at me. . . . I'm sure all that reading's bad for your eyes. . . ."

"It ain't. . . ."

"My dad used to say that on'y fools read books, because they'd such a lot to learn. . . ."

"He on'y said that because he didn't know how to read. He was jealous, if you ask me."

"No need to be jealous of the rammel you stuff your big head with. . . ."

"Look, why don't *you* get a book, duck? . . ."

"I've got more sense; and too much to do."

"Well let me read, anyway, wain't you? It's an interesting book, and I'm tired. . . ."

"Tired? You're allus tired. . . . Tired Tim! You ought do some real

work for a change instead of walking the streets with that daft post bag.
... You booky bastard ... nowt but books, books, books, you bleddy
dead-'ead." (82)

Kathy's rebuke is crude but justified, for she recognizes that her
husband has all but abandoned reality. Sillitoe usually regards cultural
awareness as the means of escape from the monotonous life of the
laboring class. But that is not the case in this story, for what the
postman seeks is not a more intense and realistic comprehension of life,
which Sillitoe seems to regard as the end function of literature; instead,
Harry is reading of "the hot possessive world of India," which
represents the realm of romance. His passivity and escapism have led
him to exchange life for life illusion.

Finding the indifference of her husband too much to bear, Kathy
departs with a house painter with whom she has been "knocking-on"
for about a year. Harry's reaction reveals an important aspect of his
personality: "No one knew where they'd skipped off to exactly,
probably imagining that I wanted to chase after them. But the idea
never occured to me. In any case what was I to do? Knock him flat and
drag Kathy back by the hair? Not likely" (83). He describes himself as
"the sort of bloke that doesn't get ruffled at anything." (80); his
existence during Kathy's absence consists of making his rounds, reading
at night, playing checkers at the club, or having a slow half-pint at the
pub up the street. As he surmises, "it wasn't a bad life. It might have
been a bit lonely, but at least it was peaceful, and it got as I didn't mind
it, one way or the other" (84).

The insidious thing about Harry's approach to this problem and to
the whole matter of existence is that he is absolutely indifferent, which,
for Sillitoe, is the same as being spiritually dead. Harry's approach to
life attempts to insure that he will never be hurt, but such an existence is
nonlife. His attitude is even more harmful than the indifference of
society collectively to its members, for what is at stake here is not the
relation of one stranger to another but what should be the most
intimate human association, that of husband and wife. Sillitoe
ironically emphasizes the point by having Harry note irritably on the
day of Kathy's first return, ten years after her departure, "I'd had a
busy day on my rounds, an irritating time of it—being handed back
letters all along the line, hearing that people had left and no one had
any idea where they'd moved to ..." (84-85).

Just before Kathy returns, Harry, who is standing in the back yard
smoking his pipe, is about to return to "a book about Brazil." He finds

seeing his wife after ten years a "shocking" experience but, at the same time, a revealing one. He observes, "I was neither glad nor happy to see her, but maybe that's what shock does, because I was surprised, that I will say. Not that I never expected to see her again, but you know how it is, I'd just forgotten her somehow" (85). They sit down together, turn over the threadbare recollections of their past existence, and are surprised to find themselves falling into the old patterns of speech; but they only mention in passing their former difficulty: "You never was very excitable, was you, Harry? . . . You should have been . . . then we might have hit it off a bit better" (88). He replies simply, "Too late now. . . . I was never one for rows and trouble, you know that. Peace is more my line" (88).

The basic problem in their relationship is represented in the picture from which the story draws its title. The painting is associated with both the pleasures and pains of their past: "It was one of a set that Kathy's brother had given us as a wedding present, the other two having been smashed up in another argument that we'd had" (87). In contrast to the stormy nature of their marriage, the picture suggests calm beauty; it portrays a vessel "brown and rusty with sails half spread in a bleak sunrise, not far from the beach along which a woman walked bearing a basket of fish on her shoulder" (87). Such harmony can be painted, framed, and hung on a wall; but, the story suggests, it can not be attained in life. When Kathy remarks upon the beauty of the picture "as though she'd never wanted anything so much in her life," Harry gives it to her with an indifference not far removed from his attitude toward her leaving him: "What does a picture more or less in the house matter? And what does it mean to me, anyway?" (91). After she has left, he notes, "it didn't take me long to get back to my book" (91).

The next day on his rounds he comes across the picture in a pawnshop window, looking at him "from the wreckage of other lives." He redeems it and mistakenly concludes that the objective of her action was to procure enough money for three pints of beer. Her subsequent visits cause him, however, to change his opinion and to reconsider her motivation. Neither mentions the incident, but on Kathy's future visits—regularly, each Thursday—she asks first for a small dole for beer and then comments on the beauty of the picture and hints "how nice it would be if she had it." She is not asking for the picture simply to exchange it for money, any more than she asks for money for beer out of necessity; as he well knows, "she could claim some sort of allowance from me—for we were still legally married—instead of coming to borrow a half-crown" (95). The borrowings are a gesture of dependence, while the request for the picture is essentially an attempt to destroy the last vestige of what Harry's indifference has already destroyed. As her husband recognizes, "I don't think she wanted the picture especially to see and get money, or to hang in her own house; only to have the pleasure of pawning it, to have someone else buy it so that it wouldn't belong to either of us any more" (97).

The visits continue for six years. Apparently, neither entertains the idea that they might resume their marriage as before; nor, apparently, do the weekly meetings consist of anything more than sitting over a cup of tea, looking at the fire, and exchanging enough talk to keep the silence from closing in about them. Finally, in the sixth year of her visits, she asks him for the painting "directly"; and he goes through the ritual, as before, of dusting, wrapping, and tying it for her. She pawns it again; but he does not trouble to redeem it again. At this point, Sillitoe fuses reality and illusion in a harsh manner. Harry receives word that Kathy has been run down by a lorry and "knocked all to bits." When he goes to the hospital to identify the body, he notes, "Among the things of hers they showed me was the fishing-boat picture, but it was so broken up and smeared with blood that I hardly recognized it. I burned it in the roaring flames of the firegrate last night" (98).

This story, like "On Saturday Afternoon," is a study of self-discovery, with the difference that, in this case, the narrator comes to realize not that he has an indomitable spirit and a determination to endure but that he is among those who have died spiritually by avoiding reality: "And looking at these few old pictures stacked in the back of my mind I began to realize that I should never have let them go, and that I shouldn't have let Kathy go either. Something told me I'd been daft and dead to do it, and as my rotten luck would have it it was the word dead more than daft that stuck in my mind, and still sticks there like the spinebone of a cod or conger eel, driving me potty sometimes when I lay of a night in bed thinking" (99).

The broader question that Sillitoe is trying to get at in this story is, "What has this life meant?" The regrettable answer, in this case, is "nothing." As Harry concludes, "I began to believe there was no point in my life—became even too far gone to turn religious or go on the booze. Why had I lived? I wondered. I can't see anything for it" (99). His early conclusion concerning their married life—"it was too much like suffering"—has undergone an important revision: "at the worst minutes of my midnight emptiness I'd think less of myself and more of Kathy, see her as suffering in a far rottener way than ever I'd done, and it would come to me—though working only as long as aspirin pitted against an incurable headache—that the object of my having been alive was that in some small way I'd helped Kathy through her life" (99). Harry has come to grips with an important aspect of the human condition; but, when the thought process begins this late in life, it is painful and not always restorative. Lapsing into despair, Harry seemingly echoes Hemingway's lost-generation characters when he says: "I was born dead, I keep telling myself. Everybody's dead, I answer. So they are, I maintain, but then most of them know it like I'm beginning to do, and it's a bloody shame that this has come to me at last when I could least do with it, and when it's too bloody late to get anything but bad from it" (99).

Quite obviously, as far as Sillitoe is concerned, there is a point beyond which a man cannot salvage his life, the postman has reached that point. The basic error of his existence was passivity, a willful abnegation of life, which produces a less obvious but no less effective destruction of the life spirit than violent suicide is. As in the existentialist hell of Sartre's "No Exit," life becomes for Sillitoe's narrator a matter of reviewing the meaning of the past, with the difference being that his character Harry reaches a bitter, but accurate, understanding: "Then optimism rides out of the darkness like a knight in armour. If you loved her . . . (of course I bloody-well did) . . . then you both did the only thing possible if it was to be remembered as love. Now didn't you? Knight in armour goes back into blackness. Yes, I cry, but neither of us *did anything about it,* and that's the trouble" (99). The man who has through passivity and indifference avoided the suffering of life must eventually face his "hell" in the realization that the events of the present finally become the memories of the past, which the mind is incapable of either revising or escaping.

VI *Human Dignity and Social Anarchy:* *"The Loneliness of the Long-distance Runner"*

"The Loneliness of the Long-distance Runner" has engaged the attention of most of the critics who have dealt with Sillitoe's works.[4] While there is general agreement that it is one of the best British short novels published in recent years, the interpretations given it have generated some surprising critical conflicts. One scholar submits that the purpose of the story is to depict the "moral decay" of the hero, Colin Smith: "he is lonely, too, because he lives his life according to a 'code' that denies him any joy in life, a 'code' that consists, in fact, of the denial of the ordinary human pleasures." He concludes, "we are led into seeing that *all* of Smith's beliefs have been false. . . ." [5] Another critic who presents a contradictory reading, explains that Colin Smith attains " 'honesty' in all its fullness. And at this moment when truth is fully apprehended, the runner's kinship with humanity (corollary of the liberation and the attainment) as distinct from his former alienation from it, is decisively established. It is almost a Christlike passion, for a tragically deluded society suicidally hostile to life. . . ." [6] While such interpretations may be defensible, Sillitoe's subsequent publications, including the screenplay of "The Loneliness of the Long-distance Runner," which he prepared for Woodfall Film Productions Ltd., suggest that neither is the reading intended by the author.

"The Loneliness of the Long-distance Runner" is written in a tradition in English fiction which dates at least from Elizabethan times, in the works of Robert Greene, Thomas Nashe, Thomas Deloney—the rogue's tale or the thief's autobiography. These works have traditionally justified their existence by purporting to serve two functions: to allow the reader to learn the tricks of outlaws so that he may avoid falling prey to them, and to lead the reader to virtue through the terrible example of its opposite. The moral in many instances is delineated by the repentant criminal himself. Sillitoe's criminal in this story is not repentant, and the moral of the tale is not so simple as to promote the cause of virtue as opposed to vice. Defoe, in his thief's autobiography, *Moll Flanders,* satisfies our moral sense by having Moll earnestly repent her past crimes; he maintains our interest by showing how Moll survives physically through cunning. In contrast to Defoe, Sillitoe offends our moral sense by having his thief stubbornly refuse repentance; but he maintains our interest by showing how the man keeps his integrity while he is under the physical and legal authority of those whom he despises. In so doing, Sillitoe has reversed the formula of the popular crime tale of fiction, wherein the reader vicariously enjoys witnessing the exploits of the outlaw and then has the morally reassuring pleasure of seeing the doors of the prison close upon him. Sillitoe begins his tale in prison, and he ends it before the doors have opened again; indeed, he leaves us with the unsettling realization that when the doors do open, the criminal will be released unreformed.

Insofar as Sillitoe's works are dominated by any one theme, that theme is rebellion. Especially in his later novels and short stories, he presents his heroes, who, with few exceptions, are members of the laboring class, rebelling against those mainstays of proletarian literature of the 1930's, oppressive management and Conservative politicians. To those who regard the subjects as anachronistic in the present decade, Sillitoe might assert, as he did in an essay on contemporary British social conditions, "In England there are half a million people out of work, and ten times that number living in real poverty, what I would call below the telly-line, as well as below the bread-line. The gap between the very poor and the normal rich is wider than it has ever been." [7] Nevertheless, while the equalitarian society which Sillitoe desires is far from an actuality, the theme of rebellion is at best somewhat muddled for a "working-class" novelist, which Sillitoe is, in a country with a Socialist Labour government during a time of comparative prosperity. The conflict, however, can be clearly defined once again by a writer of Sillitoe's predilections if he places his character in physical bondage. For this reason, "The Loneliness of the Long-distance Runner" has proved to be one of Sillitoe's most successful explorations of the theme of rebellion.

The story is related in the first person by Colin Smith (the first name is given in the filmscript, but not in the short story), who tells of a theft which he has committed, his imprisonment in Essex Borstal, his decision to lose deliberately a long-distance race, and his hatred of prison officials. We may be tempted to justify Smith's crime, as Professor Denny does, in terms of his "unfortunate home background (working-class insecurity, slum life, unemployment, periodic want) "; [8] but it is rather embarrassing to attempt to do so in relation to the facts of the story. The crime was not committed out of economic necessity; for after Smith's father died of cancer, the factory where he had been employed paid the family five hundred pounds in insurance benefits; as Smith explains, "how could any of us go to work after that?" (21). Sillitoe's sympathies are with the poor, but he does not pretend, in this story at least, that the 1950's are the 1930's.

Smith is unemployed, therefore, because he does not want employment. He commits the crime—stealing a bakery cashbox—not out of necessity, but out of choice. Moreover, he is utterly without a sense of remorse or guilt: "I don't say to myself: 'You shouldn't have done the job and then you'd have stayed away from Borstal'; no, what I ram into my runner-brain is that my luck had no right to scram just when I was on my way to making the coppers think I hadn't done the job after all" (20). The matter which the story presents is not the question of whether or not Smith is guilty or innocent. When the crime has been committed, his guilt determined, and the sentence passed, the social questions of guilt, innocence, and responsibility regarding the theft are no longer the central issue; they have, in effect, been settled. The subject of the story then becomes a presentation of the more complex conflict between the captive and his keepers.

Smith has not been assigned to a prison but to a Borstal, designed especially for young offenders and intended to rehabilitate them for a useful life upon release. Officially, the essence of the system is, "that the young person under training is to be regarded as 'a living organism ... with a life and character of his own. The task is not to break or knead him into shape, but to stimulate some power within to regulate conduct aright. ... It follows, therefore, that the men and women engaged in his training have first to know him, outside and inside, learning a little more each day about him.' " [9]

Ironically, Smith's most tenable complaint against the governor of his Borstal is stated as follows: "I'm not a race horse at all. ... I'm a human being and I've got thoughts and secrets and bloody life inside me that he doesn't know is there ..." (13). As in most human endeavors, practice falls short of theory in the Borstals; and Sillitoe's purpose is to explore the nature of the failure. But the analysis is not objective: Smith does not conceive that he is in any way in error; he tells his story, not the governor's. He does, however, carefully indicate the failure of this particular attempt at rehabilitation. The officials depicted in the story perform competently the duty of providing for the physical necessities of their charges, but their actions clearly indicate that they have little interest in them as human beings. The governor in charge of Essex Borstal is most concerned with winning the field competition between the Borstals of all of England in the annual cross-country running match. His primary purpose seems to be to promote his own professional prestige by using Smith's unusual abilities as a long-distance runner.[10] From Smith's point of view, such an act—using another man's talents—is more insidiously criminal than his own—stealing a man's wealth. Smith does not pretend that stealing is not theft, but the governor pretends that his actions are motivated by a desire to improve his prisoners: "We want hard honest work and we want good athletics. ... And if you give us both these things you can be sure we'll do right by you and send you back into the world an honest man" (10). That is to say, the governor will teach him the art of appearing to be honest.

This particular type of dishonesty, of pretending to feel what one does not, is what Smith succeeds in avoiding but what his moral exemplars willingly perform. What Smith recognizes is that "honesty" is not an absolute term: "another thing people like the governor will never understand is that I *am* honest, that I've never been anything else but honest, and that I'll always be honest. Sounds funny. But it's true because I know what honest means according to me and he only knows what it means according to him" (15). The moral inversion in this story is not the simple and obvious one commonly found in proletarian social-thesis fiction in which the "haves" are flagrantly, but legally, dishonest and those convicted of crimes are either innocent or perform their acts out of necessity for physical survival. Smith, who is quite guilty of breaking the laws of his society, does not break the laws which he feels constitute a man's humanity. In consequence, the matter of "existing" or "not existing" in this story operates on a moral rather than on a physical plane.

As G. S. Fraser has observed, Sillitoe's "view of working-class life is classical and tragic: you cannot win, but you can fight." [11] The theme of the tale is the ancient Aeschylean one—an indomitable will pitted against an overwhelming force; but Sillitoe has rendered it in an antisocial, nihilistic context. From Smith's point of view, the basis of the moral and social order, as he has experienced it, is "cunning": it is "what counts in this life" (7). What he means by "cunning," as we learn, is not simply a talent for animal survival in terms of a jungle existence, for both the stakes and the means of survival are more subtle than that. What is at issue is not food, but human will.

The matter of choice or will or spirited selfhood is associated in Smith's mind with life itself. His own position is clear; it is the rest of mankind, even the "outlaws," that he is not sure about. Consequently, he feels alternately like "the first and the last man on the world." As he explains, "I feel like the last man in the world because I think that all those three hundred sleepers behind me are dead. They sleep so well I think that every scruffy head's kicked the bucket in the night and I'm the only one left, and when I look out into the bushes and frozen ponds I have the feeling that it's going to get colder and colder until everything I can see, meaning my red arms as well, is going to be covered with a thousand miles of ice, all the earth, right up to the sky and over every bit of land and sea" (9).

Dante used ice in the ninth circle of the *Inferno* as a punishment for the traitorous to various political and familial obligations; Sillitoe uses it to represent a traitorous act of a more insidious kind. The icy scene which Smith envisions represents appropriately a massive death of the human spirit, the failure of all mankind. Smith defines the second part of the analogy—his feeling of being the "first man on earth"—in terms of his own circumstances, without relation to others: "I feel like the first man because I've hardly got a stitch on and am sent against the frozen fields in a shimmy and shorts—even the first poor bastard dropped on to the earth in midwinter knew how to make a suit of leaves, or how to skin a pterodactyl for a topcoat" (8). But "first" does not define well in terms of itself, for it necessarily implies extension in time and number, so Smith adds to his explanation. The psychological state of feeling that one is the "first" man on earth differs from its contrary in that, when one is first, "Everything's dead, but good, because it's dead before coming alive, not dead after being alive" (11). What Smith hopes will come alive are the "three hundred sleepers"; but, even if they do not, his own task lies before him, unchanged. For Smith, the difference between being the "first and the last man on the world" is hypothetical, not actual. Smith's consciousness and his sense of dignity remain absolute, even though the scale of the rest of humanity may fluctuate and vary.

This point about honesty and primal will is underscored during a practice session sometime before the actual running of the race. Far out in the countryside, where Smith has reached the halfway point of the course near a "sunken lane," the setting becomes primal, suggesting a time antedating man and his particular moral and social consciousness. Sillitoe has his long-distance runner associate himself with a creature from the Mesozoic era, an extinct flying reptile which appeared, flourished, and expired more than one hundred million years before the appearance of man. Each time Smith makes his rounds, he follows an impulse to hurl himself down a "steep bush-covered bank and into the sunken lane, when there's still not a soul in sight . . ." (19). While he recognizes the danger, the impulse to perform the act is irresistible: "I can't not do it because it's the only risk I take and the only excitement I ever get, flying flat-out like one of them pterodactyls from the 'Lost World' I once heard on the wireless, crazy like a cut-balled cockerel, scratching myself to bits and almost letting myself go but not quite" (19).

The episode suggests a type of primal and instinctual will to survive in man that transcends all his notions of morality and all social law. This "instinct" seems to be more fundamental and innate than anything produced by cognition; for, as Smith describes the particular pleasure which he finds in the experience, "It's the most wonderful minute because there's not one thought or word or picture of anything in my head while I'm going down. I'm empty, as empty as I was before I was born, and I don't let myself go, I suppose, because whatever it is that's farthest down inside don't want me to die or hurt myself bad" (19).

The same quality that's "farthest down inside" forbids him to surrender his will to his captors, for that would involve a death of spirit.

For this reason, Smith, in the most intense scene in the story, intentionally loses the race; he stops short of the finish line where the governor and other officials can see him marking time as the other runners at last catch up and pass him. What Smith recognizes is that the governor's race is not *his* race, nor is any contest arranged by captors for their captives. What Smith does not recognize is that the race which needs to be won by both sides is one of comprehension.

The author inevitably acts as judge, whether overtly (as Henry Fielding preferred to do), or reticently yet implicitly, as Sillitoe does here. Smith has received one trial, conducted by society's judge and jury; he receives another one conducted by the author. The difference between the inquiries is that society asks what the accused will say publicly that may bear relevance to legality and morality; Sillitoe asks what Smith thinks when he is alone. In so doing, the author conveys with superb artistry the psychology of a recalcitrant mind. The point of the story, however, as a solution to society's problems, is simply nihilistic.

The Borstal system described in the story does not succeed because at its base is a failure of understanding. The "in-laws" do not understand the "out-laws"; and, despite Smith's claim that he can "see further into" the governor than the governor can see into him, Smith sees with a jaundiced eye. The central problem is that both Smith and the governor make the mistake of assuming that a classification of humanity according to the terms "in-law" and "out-law" is in any sense meaningful. What the story suggests, although perhaps not intentionally, is that such simplistic categorizing is at the base of much human agony.

The art of fiction is one means of promoting understanding between individuals, and this story can convey to the governor and to us, if we are willing to listen, what the "out-law" point of view is. Communication, however, is complicated by the fact that the reader is "they," a person who must have the nature of prison life explained to him, and who, moreover, is morally and socially opposed to the narrator: "And there *are* thousands of them, all over the poxeaten country, in shops, offices, railway stations, cars, houses, pubs—In-law blokes like you and them, all on the watch for Out-law blokes like me and us—and waiting to 'phone for the coppers as soon as we make a false move" (10). The narrator assumes that the audience is composed of those who have not, heretofore, comprehended the motivations behind his actions. He believes, moreover, that the failure of communication is irremediable: "they don't see eye to eye with us and we don't see eye to eye with them, so that's how it stands and how it will always stand" (8).

We are thus led into a philosophical and sociological cul-de-sac. We may feel—by way of justifying the author's apparent sympathy with Smith's position, and the impasse to which it leads—that if there is among criminals an incorrigible attitude, then it is Sillitoe's obligation, as a writer of realistic fiction, to convey the attitude to us accurately in his portrayal of such men. It is what we as readers ought to hear, even if we would prefer to be told that reform schools make people first contrite and then obedient and lawful. On the other hand, we may feel, as Professor Hurrell does, that no justification is necessary, in that the reader is at last "led into seeing that *all* of Smith's beliefs have been false. . . ." Early in Sillitoe's career (when in fact Professor Hurrell's article was written), such an interpretation would have been vulnerable but defensible since the first-person narrative of the story leaves the author's position technically indeterminate. At the present time, it would be a mistake to suggest that Sillitoe intended Smith's views to be read as "false." In an essay on the circumstances of the writer in the modern age, for example, Sillitoe is as pessimistic as Smith regarding the possibility of communication between opposing factions—in this instance, between what he calls writers of the Left (such as himself) and writers of the Right (who are the "mouthpiece of government and ideology," including party Soviet writers): "For the purpose of this argument I will call the writer who is content with the society he lives in a man of the Right, and a writer who is by his nature against society I will call a man of the Left. . . . In writing a man of the Left is not a member of the opposition, which implies similarity in basic ideas and the possibility of becoming allies, but a revolutionary, for the Left and Right of literature that I have in mind can never meet for compromise." [12] Such a statement leaves little doubt concerning the author's position.

"The Loneliness of the Long-distance Runner" contained the seeds of the revolutionary philosophy which eventually attained full growth in Sillitoe's works. At the base of his moral perspective is the conviction expressed by Smith that those who are in accord with the present organization of society "don't see eye to eye with us and we don't see eye to eye with them, so that's how it stands and how it will always stand" (8). The position permits two possible conclusions: an impasse, as I have suggested, or revolution, which is the path that Sillitoe has chosen. Smith makes the point with brutal clarity: "in the end the governor is going to be doomed while blokes like me will take the pickings of his roasted bones and dance like maniacs around his Borstal's ruins" (46).

At the time the story was published, it seemed, as we have noted, to some readers that Smith's views were clearly intended to be read as "false"; to others, such as Professor Denny, that Smith evidences an "almost Christ-like passion, for a tragically deluded society" (certainly a most ingenious reading); and to perhaps the majority of readers that Sillitoe had produced a remarkable and sympathetic portrait of a recalcitrant, revolutionary young man whose extreme views were not necessarily those of the author. As subsequent chapters of this study demonstrate, Sillitoe's later publications (and his first novel as well) suggest that Smith's views and Sillitoe's are virtually the same. Nevertheless, "The Loneliness of the Long-distance Runner" remains a powerful expression of the necessity of human dignity; it is, indeed, an exemplum of the forcefulness with which the human will is capable of sustaining itself.

The necessity of human dignity which the story implies, however, has traditionally been counterbalanced within the consciousness of Western civilization by an equally strong sense of the necessity of human order. We are faced, quite simply, with the ancient problem of balancing any individual's concept of human freedom against the inevitable restriction of freedom necessitated by living with others in society. The tale suggests, whether intentionally or not, that the "governors" of the world, who are the instruments of social order, must come to know that order is not in itself an end; that one may establish a well-ordered colony of animals through systems of force and of punishment and reward, with a resultant civilization hardly worthy of the name. Conversely, what the "Smiths" of the world must recognize is that conceptions of human dignity are not the prerogative of any one social class—and that anarchy and social chaos are less likely to lead to freedom than to tyranny.

VII *"The Decline and Fall of Frankie Buller"*

In "The Decline and Fall of Frankie Buller," the last story in *The Loneliness of the Long-distance Runner* and, in part, the author's epilogue to the reader, we are brought inside the author's study, "in the first-floor flat of a ramshackle Majorcan house" (156); and we observe his eyes pass along the rows of books which surround him while he imagines the thoughts of occasional visitors who see the copies of

Homer's works in the original and a Greek lexicon and imagine that the author reads Greek. He does not, he informs us; nor has he read all of the twelve-volume set of Proust. The works of Euripides, Shakespeare, and Dostoevsky are there, as are James G. Frazer's *The Golden Bough*, the Holy Bible, and "a dozen mouldering Baedekers." The works call to his mind a time before he "ever saw these books, or any book at all"; and he reflects upon the impossibility of undoing the changes that reading has wrought upon his mentality: "You can't wind back the clock that sits grinning on the marble shelf. You can't even smash its face in and forget it" (156). Still, it is possible at times to turn back through the memory to the time of childhood. The sound of a cuckoo, "the soft, sharp, fluting whistle," accomplishes this return for the author, taking him back to the time of his life when he knew the title character, Frankie Buller.

The story is of a make-believe war, and the armies are composed of the rag-tag children of the slums of Nottingham. The tone of the story is serious, and the style is closer to that of a nostalgic sociological document than of fiction. Here is no colorfully dialectal narrator, as in the "Disgrace of Jim Scarfedale" or "On Saturday Afternoon"; instead, the author reflects soberly upon his own past and that of others who sprang from the same environment. When Sillitoe was twelve, Frankie Buller was somewhere between twenty and twenty-five years of age; in bodily strength, he was a full-grown man; in intellect, a child. Instead of working in the factories or entering the army like the other young men of his age, he served as the "sergeant-major" of a group of twelve-year-olds which included Sillitoe and other boys from the neighborhoods. Armed with a spear (a six-foot railing) and a shield (a dustbin lid), he led his combatants in "wars" against groups of other slum children from the nearby housing estate. One battle is described in full, and Sillitoe re-creates vividly the flanking movements, the entrenchments, the hurling of stones by both sides, and the final charge up a railroad embankment with Frankie in the lead, brandishing shield and spear and succeeding at last with his followers in routing the rival gang. The tale sketches Frankie's vandalism, his futile flirtatious behavior with the girls of the tobacco factory, and his final act of assault (hitting a railwayman on the head with a bottle), which leads him into trouble with the police.

The story then skips forward ten years, when Sillitoe had completed his own term in the armed services in Malaya and had turned to the craft of writing. Having produced an effectively nostalgic recollection throughout most of the tale, the author at last gives himself over to anger. Frankie Buller, having attacked and injured his own father, has been subjected to shock treatments. When Sillitoe learns this, he turns his wrath upon the "conscientious-scientific-methodical probers" who have harmed the "immense subterranean reservoir of his inspired mind" (174-76). Sillitoe notes, "I wanted power in me to tear down those white-smocked mad interferers with Frankie's coal-forest world, wanted to wipe out their hate and presumption" (174).

Sillitoe's anger is perhaps understandable—he would inevitably experience a sense of futility and helplessness upon encountering this debilitated figure from his childhood—but his hatred for the doctors who have performed the shock treatment upon Frankie Buller also reveals a degree of irrationality. They have clearly become, in his mind, a part of the hated Establishment. In "The Loneliness of the Long-distance Runner," Smith's hatred of the "in-laws" may or may not be justifiable in terms of his own experience; but it is esthetically admissible because he is a fictional character. In "The Decline and Fall of Frankie Buller," the narrator is Alan Sillitoe; and he reveals a fundamental hatred which in his later writing becomes a more dominant concern than the creation of artistic fiction.

Most of the stories which appeared in *The Loneliness of the Long-distance Runner* evidenced that Sillitoe possessed the potential to become a major author. The fine psychological analyses of his Nottingham youths, the skillful rendering of the environment of the factory districts, and the realistic portrayal of marital conflicts demonstrated that Sillitoe had the insight and the talent necessary for the performance of his craft. The stories indicated also that Sillitoe's best work would reflect his own particular sense of man's struggle against fate—as in "On Saturday Afternoon" and "The Loneliness of the Long-distance Runner." In those stories, the protagonists are circumscribed not merely by economic and social forces but by what amounts to an indifferent universe. As in such great comic epics as Cervantes's *Don Quixote*, Fielding's *Tom Jones*, Sterne's *Tristram Shandy*, and Voltaire's *Candide*, we sense that man has laughter and courage on his side, whereas the universe has simply brute force. Man may be beaten, but he will not be defeated. This message—that man can endure—gives Sillitoe's best writing a significance beyond the political and social issues of the moment.

CHAPTER 3

The Ragman's Daughter

THE seven stories in Sillitoe's second collection, *The Ragman's Daughter,* were written at Hertfordshire and Notting Hill Gate (London) between 1959 and 1962 after the success of *Saturday Night and Sunday Morning* and *The Loneliness of the Long-distance Runner* had ended Sillitoe's apprenticeship as an unpublished author. The change in Sillitoe's professional fortune seems to be reflected in the tone of these later stories. The author is even less conciliatory toward those of his readers who may be members of the Establishment, and his stories are more consistently concerned with the conflict between the "haves" and "have-nots." The tales in the second collection need not be discussed in as much detail as the earlier stories, but something of the content of six of them should be suggested. The stories are treated in the order of their appearance in the collection.

I "The Ragman's Daughter"

The title story represents a return to the themes presented in "The Loneliness of the Long-distance Runner," particularly the classic and tragic theme of man as a fated being. Sillitoe again demonstrates his virtuosity in conveying the attitudes of a man hostile to the structure of established society. As in "The Loneliness of the Long-distance Runner," the story is told in the first person by an unrepentant thief who recounts events which took place in his youth. As the story opens, the unnamed narrator begins by expressing his pessimistic attitude toward luck and God. Having just been searched by the police, he observes: "That's life. I was lucky my suitcase had nothing but air in it. Sometimes I walk out with a box of butter and cheese from the warehouse I work at, but for once that no-good God was on my side—trying to make up for the times he's stabbed me in the back maybe" (7). This stance marks a new direction in Sillitoe's conception of man's fate. In addition to being trapped within the social "system," man is subject to a capricious and indifferent deity.

Noticeable also is an increased disenchantment with the capitalist system and property ownership. The narrator recalls that in an infants' school, "They gave us cardboard coins to play with, pennies, shillings, half-crowns, stiff and almost hard to bend, that we were supposed to exchange for bricks and pieces of chalk. This lesson was called Buying and Selling. Even at the time I remember that there was something not right about the game . . ." (8). When he grows older and has become an accomplished thief of cars, watches, suits, and a variety of other goods, he recognizes that he really cares nothing about possessing the stolen items. In fact, he customarily drops them over Trent bridge to hear the sound they make as they fall into the river below.

This admission leads to an important passage in which the narrator rejects all but an equalitarian society: "What I'd like, believe it or not, is to live in a country where I didn't like thieving and where I didn't want to thieve, a place where everybody felt the same way because they all had only the same as everyone else—even if it wasn't much. Jail is a place like this, though it's not the one I'd find agreeable because you aren't free there. The place that fills my mind would be the same as in jail because everybody would have the same, but being free as well they wouldn't want to nick what bit each had got" (10). This passage supports the dominant theme of the story: that man, who conceives what he cannot achieve, in vain creates illusions to escape reality.

Smith, the long-distance runner, rejected any hope of illusory escape, saying: "I know every minute of my life that a big boot is always likely to smash any nice picnic I might be barmy and dishonest enough to make for myself" (18). But the narrator of this story, who has fallen in love with a young girl named Doris, whom he thinks of as "Lady Luck," imagines a fanciful escape with her from all problems of the world. He pictures the two of them riding horseback,

overland to Langley Mill and Matlock Bath without using a road once, the pair of us making a fine silhouette on some lonely skyline. Then as on the films we'd wind our way far down into the valley and get lodgings at a pub or farmhouse. Bit by bit we'd edge to Scotland and maybe at the end of all our long wanderings by horse we'd get a job as man and wife working a lighthouse. Set on a rock far out at sea, the waves would bash at it like mountains of snow, and we'd keep the lights going, still loving each other and happy even though we hadn't had a letter or lettuce in six months. (21)

Sillitoe has a habit of introducing such illusory fantasies only to make the inevitable fall to reality the more jarring. For a time, the narrator and Doris lead their conception of an idyllic existence, combining theft with love, and enjoying pleasurable rides through the countryside on a motorbike. However, even in the moments of their greatest happiness, there are natural but ominous forebodings. The narrator observes that from a distance, even slag heaps look "pale blue" and alluring in the summer, but when one approaches more closely, they become "grey and useless and scabby, too real to look good anymore" (25). The same description applies to the fantasies which man creates to sustain himself in adversity.

The narrator's conviction that man is a creature bandied about by the winds of fate is expressed in the following passage. He suddenly recalls a childhood game in which several boys hold cigarette lighters up to the wind to see which one will stay lit the longest. The narrator voices his stoic pessimism by observing that, although the game was thrilling, "you can't help but lose by it in the end. . . . Sooner or later every lighter goes out or gives in; or a wind in jackboots jumps from around the corner and kicks it flat—and you get caught under the avalanche of the falling world" (26). The close kinship of this attitude with that of Classical Greek tragedy is apparent. Every man is the subject of fate or chance, and he is more likely to be rewarded with defeat than with victory.

The theme is reinforced by an underlying current of irony in the story. The narrator, who dedicates himself to stealing, has no interest in possessing the stolen objects. His companion Doris, as the daughter of a wealthy scrap dealer, has no practical reason for stealing. While both wish to avoid detection, both make detection inevitable by their frivolous acts. In one instance, the narrator pastes stolen postage stamps on the corner of every building between the site of the robbery and his home; in another, Doris insists on turning on the lights in a darkened shoestore in order to select a pair of shoes. This act leads to the arrest and three years' imprisonment of her companion. While he is serving the term, she gives birth to his son, marries a garage mechanic, and is killed with her husband when their motorcycle collides with a gasoline truck. The ironic image which recurs to the narrator's mind is a picture of Doris riding astride a fine walking horse "the colour of best bitter' (20) passing a "bookie shop" where a man waves his winnings in the air and shouts out to her, "Hey up, Lady Luck!" (24).

The final passage of the story contains a more subtle irony not recognized by the narrator. His youthful dreams of an equalitarian society forgotten, he applauds his own good luck at having landed a job unloading huge cakes of cheese: "I'm going straight as well, working in the warehouse where they store butter and cheese. I eat like a fighting cock, and take home so much that my wife and two kids don't do bad either" (37). From Sillitoe's point of view, the fact that complacent acceptance can be engendered in such a man by a little prosperity is in itself an ironic comment on the possibility of effecting a social revolution.

II   *"The Other John Peel"*

The title of the second story, "The Other John Peel," is drawn from a nineteenth-century ballad by John Woodcock Graves, "John Peel," which begins,

> D'ye ken John Peel with his coat so gay?
> D'ye ken John Peel at the break of day?
> D'ye ken John Peel when he's far, far away
> With his hounds and his horn in the morning?
>
> For the sound of his horn brought me from my bed,
> And the cry of his hounds which he oft-times led,
> Peel's view-halloo would awaken the dead,
> Or the fox from his lair in the morning.[1]

Sillitoe's "other John Peel" is no aristocratic hunter gaily clothed, hunting in broad daylight, and making enough noise to awaken the dead. A twentieth-century English workman named Bob, he does his hunting before daylight and is careful to dress in dark clothing and to move quietly; for he poaches his game and uses an illegal, unlicensed .303 service rifle. The story is a good example of Sillitoe's attempt to adapt to contemporary terms the revolutionary spirit of a past era.

Bob is a precision machinist whose earnings permit him to own a television set, a washing machine, a house full of furniture, and an automobile; but the themes of the story would be more appropriate to a tale set in the depression. Accompanying Bob on the hunt is fellow worker Ernie, who has guided "Bob's opinion from voting Labour to a head-nodding acceptance of rough and ready Communish" (41-42). Ernie anticipates an armed revolution in England, and the discovery that Bob possesses an illegal rifle stimulates his revolutionary fervor: "There's got to be something. I feel it. We wok in a factory, don't we? Well, we're the backbone of the country, but you see, Bob, there's too many people on our backs. And it's about time they was slung off"

(42). When the Russians come, Ernie feels, he will be "liberated." Acknowledging the strangeness of such an attitude amid the prosperity described at the beginnning of the story, Sillitoe has Bob remark: "It's a good job everybody ain't like you. . . . You're a rare 'un, yo' are" (43). It becomes apparent, however, that Ernie's views are not far different from Bob's.

After the two have successfully bagged a fox, the property of aristocratic "nobs," Bob remarks: "My old man used to go poaching before the war, so we could have summat to eat. He once did a month in quod, the poor bastard. Never got a chance to enjoy real hunting, like me" (44). Thus, in a pattern common in "New Left" literature, the story circumvents the fact of contemporary prosperity by reminding the reader of the hardships of the past and by suggesting that the present generation has inherited and accepted a revolutionary obligation from its forebears. The last passage of the story obliquely suggests that the reason for revolution extends from the distant and legendary past into the present: "The road opened along a high flat ridge through a colliery village, whose grey houses still had no smoke at their chimneys. Silent headstocks to the left towered above the fenced-off coppices of Sherwood Forest" (45).

III   *"The Firebug"*

In "The Firebug," Sillitoe effectively takes us into the mind of a pyromaniac, letting the narrator describe in the first person his early inclination to steal matches from his mother, to set newpapers afire in the backyard, and finally to enkindle a large forest known as "Snakey Wood." The method of the story, as in "The Loneliness of the Long-distance Runner," "On Saturday Afternoon," and "The Fishing-Boat Picture," is to allow an irratic personality to reveal itself to the reader. Even so, the story does not escape Sillitoe's growing fascination with revolution.

The narrator, piqued at receiving punishment for listening to fire-engine sirens rather than to the teacher's lesson, remarks, "The bastard. I should have been listening to him telling us about how the army of some batchy king or other chopped up the senseless blokes of another army; then the two kings shook hands and signed a bit of paper to say things should be the same, but peaceful, and all the soldiers just sat in gangs around their little fires boiling soup and laughing, when all I thought of was how all these little fires could be joined together into a big blaze, as big as a mountain, with the two kings on top instead of that poor bloke called Guy Fawkes—just because he had a funny name" (56).

Nevertheless, the primary function of the story is to allow a man with a distorted mind to reveal it—to show his anxieties when he believes that he will be detected; his joy at seeing the glowing results of his efforts—and this narrative method Sillitoe handles best. The conclusion of the story is designed, like that of "The Loneliness of the Long-distance Runner," to leave the reader with a sense of misgiving. The "firebug" reveals that his acts were never detected and that, ultimately, he outgrew the need of them. The German bombing raids proved that "there was something bigger" than he to start fires, and courting convinced him that the best heat is generated by lovers.

IV *"The Bike"*

"The Bike," a brief story, returns to the themes of "The Loneliness of the Long-distance Runner." Colin, who is fifteen and has just quit school, reluctantly accepts the next round of responsibility and routine facing man—work—by taking a job as a sweeper in a bicycle factory. His attitudes, like those of most of Sillitoe's workers, are militant. He has seen a cinema in which Russian revolutionaries "lined everybody up and made them hold their hands out and the working blokes went up and down looking at them. Anybody whose hands was lily-white was taken away and shot. The others was O. K. Well, if that ever happened in this country, I'd be O.K. . . ." (105).

One of Colin's workmates, Bernard, is among those who would be taken away and shot in such a circumstance; for he finds stealing more pleasurable and less demanding than work. Playing upon Colin's desire for a new bicycle, Bernard sells him a stolen one. The owner repossesses the bike while Colin is in a barber shop. When the police take him to the station for questioning, Colin recognizes the irony of having been duped by one of his own class. Although he is angry at Bernard, he does not expose him as the thief because, as he explains, "I hated the coppers more and wouldn't nark on anybody, not even a dog" (111).

Class loyalty is one of the cardinal virtues in Sillitoe's system of ethics, and the police are never to be trusted, but the fact remains that Bernard is a scoundrel. Consequently, Colin takes solace in the thought that, "if there's a revolution and everybody's lined up with their hands out, Bernard's will still be lily-white, because he's a bone-idle thieving bastard—and then we'll see how he goes on; because mine won't be lily-white, I can tell you that now. And you never know, I might even

be one of the blokes picking 'em out" (112). The threat sounds
ominous, and this enthusiastic attitude toward an English revolution
does anticipate *A Tree on Fire,* but the purpose of the short story
hardly seems to be to fan the fires of insurrection. The tone is
lighthearted, and the point of the tale seems to be the simple one
common to O. Henry's stories: to demonstrate that the experiences of
man are humorously ironic.

V   *"To Be Collected"*

In "To Be Collected," Sillitoe moves to a stratum of society lower
than any that he has presented before: he depicts three brothers who
eke out an existence traveling from door to door collecting rags, papers,
and scrap. The author takes us into the consciousness of a level of
humanity even more dimly understood by most readers than the
recalcitrant outlaw mind depicted in "The Loneliness of the Long-
distance Runner." Sillitoe, as a man who, like Brian Seaton of *Key to
the Door,* grew up playing in Nottingham dump grounds among men
who scratched out their living there, seems well qualified to portray
such subjects in fiction. While we may feel uncomfortable referring to
them as "subhuman," Sillitoe does so, and justifiably; for they
comprise part of a subculture isolated from most of the technological,
cultural, and social advances of their era. They are part of those
half-million Englishmen whom Sillitoe describes as being "below the
telly-line, as well as below the bread-line." [2]

We recognize Sillitoe's meaning when he describes the difficulty of
the struggle for survival at this socio-economic level. The tools of
survival are more primitive; the odds of winning, less sure. One of the
three brothers, Donnie, regards his existence as futile: "He'd collected
nothing. Locusts and desert, he thought. Every crumb scratched and
scraped—and saw himself in the same mind maybe as those poor
enormous animals in prehistoric times come to the end of their tether
because the sun had dried up the earth—which was better than this
wet" (121). The primitive level of consciousness and the desperate
nature of existence is suggested in one idle conversation of the morning
portrayed in the story:

> "All we'll get," Bert prophesied, "is a couple of bugged-up bedticks
> that a consumptive man and wife have just pegged out on. We'll be
> lucky to get eighteen pence the two: a cup of tea and a bun each."

"That wain't keep my gang o' kids," Donnie put in. "But we'll get more than that though, Yo' see."

. . . .

"You might just as well put your head in the gas-oven and be done wi' it," Bert said.

"That wouldn't do, either," Donnie smiled. "You've got no right to talk like that. No use dying, is it?" Bert's eyes half closed at Donnie spinning things out to such a dead-end conclusion and, turning a corner, he roared into his ear:

"Wrap up. Brainless bastard"—so loud that even above the engine noise a policeman heard its subhuman command and glared into the cab to see what was the matter. (116)

Having established the nature of his characters, Sillitoe, midway in the story, heightens the suspense and focuses upon the central dramatic incident in the tale. Donnie, the most optimistic of the brothers in that he believes that "things might have been worse in a German deathcamp, and that pigswill was better than no swill at all" (116), makes a phenomenal discovery in an abandoned brick chapel. Like the whole environment in which the brothers move, the building is hostile: its windows are blocked with wooden bars wound with barbed wire, and its brick wall is topped with broken bottles embedded in concrete.

Inside, Donnie discovers a sack containing several Sten machine guns which he carries back to the truck where his brothers are waiting. The find precipitates a heated argument among the three. All are violently hostile towards the representatives of law and order, but they take out their hostility, for the most part, in fantasies of violence directed against the police. Earlier in the story, Bert, the youngest, had wished for eight machine guns mounted on their truck to use in blasting the police. Suddenly, he finds before him the means of turning fantasy into reality. Even assuming that the weapons would never be put to such a fantastic use, they represent a source of potential wealth greater than the three men could earn in a year's time; they are objects to be sold to a group such as the revolutionary Irish Republican Army. Dave, the eldest and most prudent of the brothers, recognizes, however, that even the possession of such illegal weapons carries with it the danger of arrest and imprisonment. Dave's resultant anger bewilders Donnie, who felt that he had done a good deed for them all by discovering the guns.

Against Donnie's protestations, the other two decide that the weapons must be abandoned; as a result, they drive to an isolated lake

to discard them. At this point, the story begins to operate on an
allegorical as well as a literal level. After they have thrown four of the
guns into the stagnant lake water, Donnie grabs one, loads it, and points
it at his brothers. An unbearable tension develops as Donnie expresses
in subliterate language his bitterness at always being the butt of their
jokes and at having his extraordinary find discarded because of their
fear. As Donnie hurls curses at his astounded brothers, Sillitoe conveys
effectively the sense of a long-suppressed, primitive spirit rising
suddenly to the surface, one which cannot be calmed or subdued by the
appeals to reason which Bert and Dave present. When Donnie reveals
that the brothers have always, in his eyes been the equivalent of hated
"bosses," the story becomes a quasiparable, illustrating the possible
consequences of a rebellion, not by one Donnie, but by all of his class,
and demonstrating as well the insufficiency of the force of reason to
combat it. The title, we recognize, refers also to the legacy of bitterness
which may one day be "collected" by the society which provides the
castaway articles upon which the brothers exist.

A long, tense dialogue between Donnie and the brothers ensues,
culminating in Donnie's promise to count to seven and then to kill
them. Following the slow and deliberate count, he does not shoot but
grins, explaining: "You thought I meant it, didn't you? Well I do. But if
you think I'm going to do it when you expect it though, you're both
bloody-well wrong" (141). The brothers, and the reader, realize that
there is no predicting the actions which such a mentality may produce.
As the two men grovel in fear on the ground, Donnie abruptly and
irrationally flings the gun into the water and breaks into laughter at the
spectacle his brothers present. They scuffle with him briefly; but,
afterward, the three are reconciled and drive back to town.

They experience a certain sense of brotherhood at having overcome
a potentially disastrous situation, but there is also something in the
tone of the conclusion to suggest that they have been tricked and
cheated by fate. The three have avoided destroying one another, but
their circumstance in relation to the rest of the world remains
unchanged. There is a vague awareness among them that they had a
means to wealth or revolution in their hands and threw it away. As the
eldest remarks, they have succeeded only in wasting gasoline and time.
Our last glimpse of them reminds us of their position, as Donnie relates
an incident which happened to him earlier in the morning:

"I forgot to tell you," Donnie said. "It was a scream." He laughed until
Dave told him to get on with it then. "Well, I went to this house at

Eastwood, before I found the guns, and a collier comes to the door, a great big bastard still in his helmet and pit-muck, his trousers patched and his vest in tatters. 'What do *yo'* want?' he bawls out at me. I thought he was going to smash me with the pick he's got in his hand. So I says: 'Got any old rags, mate?' And he looks at me for half a minute, then says, 'Ar, TEK ME!' and slams the door in my face." (145)

Donnie's joke, we recognize, is about himself and his three brothers. They are the castoffs of society; they realize it and have the good humor to laugh about it. But Sillitoe has suggested to his readers that these men have grievances and a potentiality for violence which society cannot long afford to ignore.

VI   *"The Good Women"*

"The Good Women," the last story, and one published originally in the *Daily Worker,* represents Sillitoe's most obvious attempt in the collection to relate the current "New Left" movement to the social conditions of the 1930's. The story opens in a jail cell where an unnamed narrator explains that he has been arrested on the preceding night for participating in a "Ban the Bomb" demonstration which took place in the 1950's in Trafalgar Square. Turning quickly from the present to the past. he recalls his own youthful rebellion against law and authority and his first acquaintance with the primary subject of the tale, Liza Atkin.

The setting of the story then becomes Nottingham during the depression, and we learn of the privations of Liza and her family, who at one point owned only a kitchen table and a portable bathtub, both of which served at night as beds. We see Liza as a woman in her thirties, the mother of two boys, working desperately to supplement the family's dole money by picking through the rubbish pits for salable objects. Even this wretched activity is thwarted by that hated representative of government penuriousness during the depression, the "means-test man," who warns Liza that her dole will be reduced if she continues to supplement it.

When the war with Germany finally brings with it work and some prosperity to those of Liza's class, the theme of the story correspondingly alters. A deserter named "Robert the Welchman" escapes to Nottingham and is hidden from the military authorities by Liza. The incident demonstrates the "New Left's" remarkable juggling of history and logic, for a British deserter in the 1950's or 1960's is, by "New

Left" standards, a man of patriotic dedication; his actions theoretically serve the cause of the Soviet block against the aligned nations of the "free world." Sillitoe's attempt to combine the past with the present is, however, somewhat illogical and anachronistic, for he must present a pro-Communist (Liza) sheltering a hero-deserter who, remarkably, refuses to fight against fascist Germany. The deserter's explanation of his action is a standard Marxian one: there is no need to oppose capitalist, Fascist Germany, for it will inevitably be brought low by "economic collapse" (161). Hitler's disastrous invasion of Russia is cited as proof of the theory, and the narrator remarks, "My head spun at such political acumen . . ." (162).

Moving forward to the early 1950's, the story depicts Liza's anguished grief as she learns of the death of her son Harry in the Korean conflict. The transition is made from rebellion against war to rebellion against capitalism, as Liza, at the age of forty-five, takes a job in a factory and becomes, as the shop steward describes her, "The apostle of industrial unrest" (174). She is drawn into the labor conflict by a resemblance which she sees between her dead son and a fiery young union leader who exhorts his coworkers to revolution: " 'It's not a raise here and a bit of an improvement there that we want—none of it'll take. It's a whole bloody change'—his wide-apart fists gave a slow forceful turning motion as if at the wheel of some great ship and making a violent alteration in its course—'a turnover from top to bottom.' " (179).

Sillitoe conveys the turbulent excitement which accompanies the striking workers as they move en masse into a square to demonstrate, and he renders with poignancy a confused but dedicated Liza standing loyally in rain-drenched streets to support the cause of her class. The story is intended to persuade the reader of the justness of the political philosophy which it conveys. Recalling nostalgically Liza's death at the age of fifty-five, the narrator makes the transition from past to present by angrily asserting: "Liza was a good woman who lived a life worth thinking about on a long night like this. If anybody ever asks me why I got hauled in by the coppers maybe I'll tell them about her" (189). In short, Sillitoe defends the politics of the "New Left" by explaining the deprivations of the 1930's to an audience too young to have known them or too prosperous and forgetful to remember them. The technique is quite similar to that in John Arden's *Serjeant Musgrave's Dance, An Unhistorical Parable*, which we discussed in Chapter 1.

The stories in *The Ragman's Daughter* seem, on the whole, less artful than those in *The Loneliness of the Long-distance Runner*. There are some successful fictional moments in "The Ragman's Daughter" and in "To Be Collected," but the stories in general lack the full development of characters and plot found in the earlier tales. Saul Maloff has noted another difficulty:

The class war in "The Ragman's Daughter" is hardly more than a kind of hoodlumism with slight quivers of ideological overtones, and the apocalyptic fantasies of universal destruction seem willed and self-indulgent. The poacher ... poaches simply because there are the rich and one poaches from the rich because—because they are *there*. And the boy who is in trouble over a stolen bike dreams of revolution, but his dream is a nasty boy's fantasy of revenge. The revolution of his fantasy is not cleansing or purifying; it is not the visionary's dream of a better world; it is more nearly a storntrooper's quasi-erotic vision of holocaust—a day when everyone will be lined up with his hand out. . . . It should be added, though, that these characters are declassed, aspiring out of their class. The "ragman" drives a maroon Jaguar; and his daughter visits her lover—with whom she breaks into factory offices for a lark—on horseback.[3]

Sillitoe's first two volumes of short stories demonstrate his virtuosity as a creator of character, as a fictional technician, and as a social commentator. With regard to Sillitoe's professional development, the two volumes also illustrate the author's growing concern with fiction as a vehicle of political protest. In *The Loneliness of the Long-distance Runner,* only the title story carries a theme of violent rebellion against the Establishment and the forces of social order, but all of the stories in the second volume, except "The Magic Box" (a tale of domestic conflict similar to "The Fishing-boat Picture"), are concerned to some degree with that theme. The gradual change of emphasis witin the short stories has a parallel, as we shall see, in Sillitoe's novels.

CHAPTER 4

Guzman, Go Home

NINE years after the publication of *The Loneliness of the Long-distance Runner,* Sillitoe's third volume of short stories appeared. There is little within the collection that is strikingly new with regard to themes or techniques; however, the tales reflect a competent artistry, and three should be discussed.

I *"The Revenge"*

In the first story in the book, "The Revenge," a factory worker, Richard, recalls his marriage, at the age of forty, to Carolyn, then thirty. The predominant theme is a recurrent one in Sillitoe's works: that marriage turns the wine of love to vinegar. At the party following the wedding ceremony, the newlyweds and their guests eat and drink heavily; Richard makes a speech, sings a song; his friends make sly remarks regarding the wedding night; there is gaiety everywhere. At last Richard ushers the last of his inebriated friends out the door and the lovers are left alone: but the ceremony, the speeches, the stacking up of gifts, and the heavy eating and drinking have so frazzled the nerves of the couple that they are unable to make love.

Somehow their humanity has gotten misplaced amid the piles of glittering gifts, which they have received: the "toasters, dinner-services and tea-sets, electric blankets, transistor radios, horseshoes and tele-grams, records and ashtrays, plastic fruit and paper flowers, kettles and bedside lights" (8). Richard, frustrated and angry, vents his wrath upon these objects, smashing them to bits with a heavy metal poker which his workmates have given him. Following this horrendous beginning, the two muddle through love for two years and then gradually fall into a pattern of apathy, indifference, and mutual destruction. Carolyn, upon bringing her husband tea each morning, asks "How do you know it isn't poisoned?" For Richard, the continuation of their relationship is ultimately a choice between social propriety and survival: "Social laws are made to be kept up to a point because they make life easier among the pain and squalor, but when you stray by mistake into a swamp you are obliged to fight for your life and get out of it. If you can't keep your dignity, then all laws have to be thrown overboard" (25).

It is Carolyn rather than Richard who throws law overboard, lacing her husband's tea with sleeping powder one morning. The mixture proves to be stupefying but not fatal, and Richard protects his wife by telling the doctors that he attempted suicide. After a disappointing session with two insensitive psychiatrists, Richard severs his relationship with his wife and with society, taking a job with a construction crew and vowing not to live again in an "impersonal chaos." The themes are familiar ones in Sillitoe's works: the mutual destruction that marriage nurtures, the dehumanizing effects of a materialistic society, and man's ultimate obligation to survive, at whatever cost. In earlier stories—"The Fishing-boat Picture," "The Loneliness of the Long-distance Runner," and "On Saturday Afternoon," for example—Sillitoe conveyed these points with greater psychological subtlety and dramatic precision.

II *"Guzman, Go Home"*

The title story of the collection, "Guzman, Go Home," is in form a frame story and a confessional. The frame depicts a young English married couple—Chris, who is a painter, his wife Jane, and their son—driving across Spain on a vacation designed to lift the "dead useless tree of London" off their nerves. As in *The Death of William Posters* and *A Tree on Fire* there is an underlying sense of frustration and dissatisfaction growing out of the fact that England in the 1960's, Under a Labour government, has not proven fertile ground for the revolution which Sillitoe anticipated in his earlier works. In Spain, Chris and his wife are conscious of "the meaning of freedom from claustrophobic and dirty London, from television and Sunday newspapers, and their middle-aged mediocre friends who talked more gibly nowadays of good restaurants than they had formerly about socialism" (138).

The story proper begins when Chris's car breaks down and a man who speaks Spanish with a German accent comes to their aid. The man, whose name is Guzman, takes the couple and their car to an automobile-repair shop which he owns; he then dominates the remainder of the story by detailing his opinions and life history to Chris over a bottle of cognac. The subjects of his monologue are varied: the merits of automobiles, the nature of human reason, the relation of the artist to politics, what Hitler meant to Germany, Guzman's own troubled present life, and a number of other topics. Guzman is personally affable, obliging, and garrulous. So pleased is he to find someone to talk with in the remote village that he is anxious to oblige Chris in every way, but he ends by alienating the Englishman.

Guzman's *apologia* takes the form of a dramatic monologue: we can surmise Chris's reactions and questions only by Guzman's acknowledgment of them. Throughout the twenty-page monologue, Guzman addresses Chris as "England," never by his first name, and one gathers that Sillitoe intends the conversation to represent an attempt by an older generation of postwar Germans to explain its past to a young generation of Englishmen.

Guzman, who has been an artist himself, begins by stating that politics and art do not mix, but he also explains the difficulty of avoiding involvement. Prewar Germany was in economic chaos; savings and investments were wiped out; people were financially ruined. Then there emerged a leader to bring the people out of chaos:

We were patriotic, England, and radical as well. Ah! It is good when all the people go forward together. . . . But you shouldn't think I like the bad things, though, about inferior races and so on. . . . It was a proud and noble time when loneliness was forgotten. It contained sensations I often spend my nights thinking about . . . the contentment of knowing a leader who pointed to me the fact that I was different from those people I had been through on my travels. He drew me together. Ah! England, at that you get more angry than if I had banged you on the shoulder like a jolly German! (156)

Despite his found memories of the "proud and noble time," Guzman has difficulty rationalizing his act of killing prisoners: "I sat down to eat. They were hungry in the snow, and I could not stop myself. . . . I thought: their life is agony. I will end it. . . . I fired my gun. My way was terrible after that, out of control. I was not rational" (166).

England, Chris, is not impressed; nor is he sympathetic when Guzman reveals his present difficulty, the fear that he is being tracked down by a young Jew who intends to bring him to trial for war crimes. Chris's only comment on Guzman's long tale is given after he and his wife depart and their car breaks down again: "That crazy Nazi . . . can't even mend a bloody car" (169). For Sillitoe, as for Chris, there is no rationale or justification for what the Germans did in World War II; their actions, in fact, demonstrate that the "highest attributes of mankind are of dubious value." As Guzman himself succinctly puts it,

"Rational and intelligent! Everybody is being rational and intelligent. What beautiful words—but they have to be kept in a case and admired . . ." (168). Richard Sterne gives the following reading of Guzman's plight and of the story's theme: "Sillitoe's point is unmistakable: our personal confusions may be mitigated by any 'system of social life' that comes to 'involve us deeply,' but there are hideous systems and involvements as well as humane ones. Through his art, Sillitoe asks us to make a choice."[1]

III *"Canals"*

"Canals" is certainly the most sensitively written story in the volume. Its subject is the pain of remembrance that comes with returning home after a ten-year absence to witness the death of one's father. The protagonist, Dick, grew up in a poor section of Nottingham, served a term in the army, and, discovering that he had a talent for formal learning, continued his schooling and became a teacher. Ten years prior to the opening of the story, he had left home, and his mother, echoing Thomas Wolfe, had said to him, "Well, you'll always be able to come back. If you can't come home again, where can you go?" (38–39). He did come home, once, four years later, but found his family so hypnotized by the television set that they could scarcely accord him a greeting. After that, he remained in London with his wife and children until notified that his father was dying of cancer.

Within three days of Dick's arrival, his father dies; an hour after his death the undertakers have removed the body, the mattress has been rolled up and set outside for the dustmen, and the bed on which the old man died has been folded back into a divan. The impersonal efficiency with which the deceased are disposed of is prelude to the larger theme of the story: the pain of consciousness occasioned by returning "home." The pain arises in part from the recognition of one's own mortality.

In the presence of our day-to-day surroundings, we tend to forget the larger stretches of time that have made up our lives; we may have seen a tree or a house for the first time ten years ago, but we also saw it a year ago and last week and yesterday, so that the tree and the house seem to be more ours—part of our distant past, perhaps, but also part of our present life, which is the only aspect of our lives we possess with any certainty. On returning home after an absence of several years, however, we observe objects—trees, buildings, canals—which belong to our past but not to our present. They are both familiar and alien to us.

They evoke memories of a time which once was ours and which arises dimly in our consciousness, but to that time we cannot return, to that self we cannot return, and there is in this a recognition of our own mortality. It is probably less our future mortality which casts a cloud over our emotions than the mortality of that past self and consciousness which is now dead.

Without stating the above in so many words, Sillitoe manages to convey these emotions in his protagonist as Dick visits pubs he had known as a young man, talks with a cousin who urges him to return "home," and at last visits with Marian, a former sweetheart who had married after Dick had enlisted in the service. Reluctant to revive the relationship and yet drawn to see her again, Dick makes his way to Marian's house, aware that "if he were a man now he would not have come back looking for her, unable to say what he wanted, whether it was love or chaos he hoped to resurrect" (52).

Sillitoe shows that the value of a direct confrontation with the past is that it forces us to abandon ambivalent attitudes and to make a conscious choice. Dick is greeted at the door by Marian's twelve-year-old son, who is mildly hostile toward this man with whom he senses he must compete for his mother's affection. After the boy has gone to bed, Marian and Dick try to pick up the thread of their past relationship, but the fifteen years have wrought changes which cannot be ignored. Dick is not eighteen now, but thirty-three, with a wife and family. Marian has been through an unhappy marriage and separation and wants no part of marriage again. Although the two make assurances that the love of each for the other still exists, no amount of reminiscing can undo the years. Dick's conclusion, thought but not spoken, is that "The past was impotent, finally, with no cleansing quality in its slow-burning fires. Yet they could never be put out because the canals that led to them were baked dry at the bottom with the rusting and tattered debris of the life you lead" (60). He recognizes, finally, that "the past is only good when what you pull up can be seen as part of the future" (62).

While most of the tales in *Guzman, Go Home* are simply comparable in quality to Sillitoe's earlier short stories, "Canals" marks a clear advance in Sillitoe's maturity as an artist. An Arthur Seaton (the hero of *Saturday Night and Sunday Morning*) would in all probability have found an opportunity for fighting and fornicating in the return home described in this story. But Sillitoe is here concerned with the uses of the past in ways that Marcel Proust and Thomas Wolfe were.

CHAPTER 5

Saturday Night and Sunday Morning

Saturday Night and Sunday Morning, written in Majorca between 1954 and 1957, was Sillitoe's first published work of fiction, and it remains his most highly praised. The acclaim accorded the novel arises partly from the fact that Sillitoe captured in this work the essence of working-class existence more successfully than he has in any subsequent work other than *Key to the Door.* John Dennis Hurrell has observed:

Saturday Night and Sunday Morning is much more than a documentary account of the life of a capstan-lathe operator in a Nottingham bicycle factory, but if it did not have that basis, it would be nothing. Sillitoe convinces us that character grows largely out of environment; all standards, moral or social, are to a major extent products of one's *milieu;* so he provides for us not just a background against which his characters function, but a true environment which has conditioned and which explains them. Out of a deep but narrow study of a man engaged in one kind of working-class activity he has achieved the universality that no self-conscious pursuit of the significant can give.[1]

I The Workingman-Rogue

The impelling force of *Saturday Night and Sunday Morning* is the protagonist, Arthur Seaton, a lathe operator in a bicycle factory, and, in his private life, a seducer and rogue. He enters the novel "dead drunk" and soon tumbles down a flight of stairs at a local public house, the "White Horse Club." The occasion of the celebration is nominally the victory of a local athletic team, but a more significant fact is that it is the end of the week, "Saturday Night," from which the first section of the novel draws its title. To Seaton, it is "one of fifty-two holidays in the slow-turning Big Wheel of the year, a violent preamble to a prostrate Sabbath. Piled-up passions were exploded on Saturday night, the effect of a week's monotonous graft in the factory was swilled out in a burst of goodwill" (4).

The passage sets forth one important theme in the novel: that the labor which Seaton performs is, from his point of view, essentially meaningless. He is only in a specialized sense a representative of the youthful members of the laboring class of contemporary Britain—no one character could do that successfully—but he does clearly represent the spirit of youthful rebellion that transcends both his social class and his particular historical moment. His actions are flamboyant (his inebriated condition is the consequence of a humorous drinking contest with a boasting sailor), but they are also infantile. At the end of Arthur's tumble down the long flight of stairs, Sillitoe describes him appropriately as "a fully-dressed and giant foetus curled up . . . on a plush-red carpet, hiding in the shadow of two aspidistras that curved out over him like arms of jungle foliage" (6). In the progress of the novel, Seaton gradually moves away from this symbolic infantile position toward greater maturity.

The novel is divided into two parts: the first twelve chapters—about four-fifths of the novel—comprise "Saturday Night"; the last four, "Sunday Morning." Part I details the nature of Seaton's work at the bicycle factory and his adulterous affair with two women: Brenda (the wife of one of his workmates) and Winnie, Brenda's sister. The affair involves a pregnancy which ends in abortion, a riotous celebration at Goose Fair, and Seaton's defeat at the hands of Winnie's soldier-husband. "Sunday Morning" traces the conclusion of Seaton's first mature relationship with a woman, the young girl Doreen to whom he is engaged to be married as the novel closes.

Sillitoe has been appropriately labeled by most reviewers and critics as a "working-class novelist." Saul Maloff notes that, "Whatever else he is, whatever the elements of anarchism in his work, Sillitoe is obsessively concerned with a single idea, the discovery of self through the discovery—or discovery anew—of class solidarity. That egregious contemporary cliché—the quest for self-discovery—has no other meaning for him, and there is no other form which that process of consolidation, of cohesion, can take than the individual's recognition of his social role and class affiliation. The reader is struck again and again by the fact that when we enter the inner recesses of Sillitoe's protagonists, these are the contents we discover there."[2] If this analysis is accurate, it may seem surprising, then, that Seaton is portrayed as having no qualms about seducing the wife of one of his workmates, Jack. Eschewing any notions of loyalty due to one of his own class, Seaton acts in a primitivistic and amoral fashion, assuming that, if a husband neglects his wife, another man will take his place. He can feel momentary pangs of conscience, can even think of telling Jack the truth about Brenda: "Out of friendship, out of the feeling of being pals. . . . It's a rotten trick, he argued to himself, to play on your mate. Just for a bit of love" (56); but he does not carry into action the thought of revealing the truth.

There are two reasons for Seaton's not telling Jack. First, Jack serves throughout the novel as a foil to Arthur. To Seaton, Jack seems "timid in many ways, a self-contained man who did not give much of himself away"; he is the sort who "never shouted or swore or boozed like a fish, or even got mad no matter how much the gaffers got on his nerves; he never opened his mind so that you could take a squint inside to see what he was made of" (40). Those are the superficial differences; the real antagonism between the two lies deeper. Seaton is a devoted individualist, particularly in his attitude toward his employers, but Jack is willing to accommodate his own desires to those of his superiors. Sillitoe connects this aspect of Jack's personality with his marital difficulties; his willingness to work on the night shift makes it easier for his wife to commit adultery. As Maloff notes, "Sillitoe's workers have the whip-hand over no one; and if one should get it—should he 'sell out,' as Jack, Brenda's husband, does, simply by aspiring to become one of 'Them'—he will go dead, and impotent; and Sillitoe punishes by cockolding him." [3]

The second reason Seaton does not hesitate to take advantage of Jack arises from Seaton's view of life as a "jungle." He is, as the novel begins, persuaded that self-interest counts most in the scheme of things. This belief is reflected in the fact that, within an hour after seducing Brenda, he can feel not only "good and generous at buying beer" for her busband but also think, that "Jack's a good bloke. It's hard luck that things stand the way they do" (56). Later in the novel, after seeing Brenda through the excruciating experience of attempting abortion by immersing herself in steaming water and drinking great quantities of gin, Seaton climbs into bed with her sister Winnie (whose soldier-husband is stationed in a foreign country) and reflects with absolute serenity of conscience: "Never had an evening begun so badly and ended so well" (101).

Such actions and attitudes clearly place Seaton in the rogue-hero tradition in English fiction that had its beginnings in the works of such Elizabethan authors as Thomas Nashe and Thomas Deloney. Following the established pattern, Seaton can revel in his misdeeds, but he must at last pay for them and learn through suffering. His punishment, which comes later in the novel, eventually leads him to a more mature attitude toward his obligations within society.

II *Labor and Rebellion*

Having suggested the nature of Arthur's use of leisure, Sillitoe next turns to the man at his work. The day for returning to the factory is to Seaton "Black Monday," a return to the "treadmill," which, as we have noted, explains in part his chaotic attempt to escape during the weekend. Indeed, his whole environment is circumscribed by the factory. Since his home is only a five-minute walk from the factory gate, its sounds and smells stay with him constantly: "Generators whined all night, and during the day giant milling machines . . . gave to the terrace a sensation of living within breathing distance of some monstrous being" (22). The factory becomes a symbol of the jungle which is largely responsible for molding Seaton's system of values. As James Gindin observes, "Some jungles are social, institutional, the codified and established representations of man's nature. The bicycle factory where Arthur works, an institution that regularizes man's struggle against his fellows, that pits foreman against manager, worker against foreman, workers against each other, is such a representation. The organized society becomes, in Sillitoe's world, the framework in which man's predatory instincts operate."[4]

Seaton regards Robboe, a man who has an office and supervises the workers, as the "enemy's scout." The attitude, Seaton realizes, is one "passed on by his father," but that inheritance is not the whole explanation of his attitudes: "Though no strong cause for open belligerence existed as in the bad days talked about, it persisted for more subtle reasons that could hardly be understood but were nevertheless felt, and Friday afternoon was a time when different species met beneath white flags, with wage packets as mediators, when those who worked in the factory were handed proof of their worth, which had increased considerably in market value since the above-mentioned cat-and-dog ideas had with reason taken root" (61).

Indeed, the economic condition of laborers in England after World War II has much improved in comparison to their prewar status, but the psychological effect of the work has remained largely unchanged. Arthur, aged twenty-one when the novel opens, has been in the factory since the age of fifteen, working continuously except for two years spent in the army. His craft requires skill, but the work is nevertheless tedious, monotonous, and mind-dulling. For a few minutes at the beginning of each day, he is aware of his actions as he performs his tasks: "Turn to chamfer, then to drill, then to blade-chamfer. Done. Take out and fit in a new piece. . . . Turn to chamfer and drill, then blade-chamfer, swing the turret until my arms are heavy and dead. Quick as lightning. Take out and fix in, shout for the trolley to take it away and bring more on, jotting down another hundred . . ." (34). This work is performed best without cognition: "The minute you stepped out of the factory gates you thought no more about your work. But the funniest thing was that neither did you think about work when you were standing at your machine. You began the day by cutting and drilling steel cylinders with care, but gradually your actions became automatic and you forgot all about the machine and the fact that you were cutting and boring the rough threading to within limits of only five-thousandths of an inch" (35).

Seaton's ambition is stifled because of his company's policy of rating the wages paid by each piece produced: if a laborer worked at maximum efficiency, that rate became the "norm"; and a new standard for pay was established. Thus, Arthur turns out only a hundred pieces rather than the four hundred that he could produce in the same period of time; and he fills his consciousness with escapist dreams, "a compatible world of pictures that passed through your mind like a magic-lantern, often in vivid and glorious loonycolour, a world where memory and imagination ran free and did acrobatic tricks with your past and with what might be your future" (36). Through such escape, Seaton avoids sinking into the dead, thought-bereft existence in which man and machine finally become indistinguishable. This situation is the insidious danger of such work, Sillitoe seems to suggest: that the mind may decay through disuse, so that life becomes a cycle of meaningless work—grinding out thousands of parts each identically alike—and of an equally self-destroying leisure: reveling in sensual pleasure in youth and then sitting mindless before a television tube in old age, as Arthur's father does. Seaton's debauched and adulterous weekends account for much that is entertaining in the novel, but Sillitoe himself is aware of the implications of such a life. "It is the story of a man," he notes, "who has his earthly bread but not his spiritual bread. He has no spiritual values because the kind of conditions he lives in do not allow him to have any."[5]

To those not yet defeated in spirit, as Arthur is not, the prospect of being trapped in a pointless existence arouses anger which, held beneath the surface, is transformed into imaginary nihilistic schemes. One after-

noon, as he begins the task of grinding out four hundred identical parts
for bicycles, he thinks:

I'll never let anybody grind me down because I'm worth as much as any
other man in the world. . . . If they said: "Look Arthur, here's a
hundred-weight of dynamite and a brand-new plunger, now blow up the
factory," then I'd do it, because that'd be something worth doing.
Action. I'd bale-out for Russia or the North Pole where I'd sit and laugh
like a horse over what I'd done, at the wonderful sight of gaffers and
machines and bikes going sky-high one wonderful moonlit night. Not
that I've got owt against 'em, but that's just how I feel now and
again. (37)

An observation which Maloff makes is appropriate: "What the guild
socialists meant by work fit for human beings has not been possible for
a long time—and no one knows it better than Sillitoe's characters. You
stay alive at the machine by dreaming of other things—women and gin
and country Sundays. And always those dreams are crossed by nightmares of violence—Sillitoe's characters oscillate between their dreams of
flight and their nightmares of entire desolation."[6] The fantasies of
destruction are part of the puerile philosphy which dominates Seaton
during the first part of the novel, but they are also a means, however
rudimentary, of maintaining some degree of selfhood. The maxim
which Arthur most frequently repeats, "It's a hard life if you don't
weaken," explains in part his resorting to the illusory scenes of
violence. An even greater temptation is to give up the struggle, efface
self, and submit at last to the system.

   Seaton strives to maintain his independence even in the most trivial
matters. For example, rather than join the other workers in drinking
the company tea, which is free but inferior, he brings his own. He
refuses to stand in line to purchase tickets for the cinema, even if it requires only five minutes, because he has never queued in his life and
does not intend to. More importantly, although he is an "angry young
man," he does not subordinate his thought to any particular political
party, as some of Sillitoe's later heroes do. It is not surprising that
Seaton dislikes Tories, but he also distrusts labor leaders, who "rob our
wage packets every week with insurance and income tax and try to tell
us it's all for our own good" (32).

   Seaton's politics, if anything, are capricious. In one election he voted
for the Communist candidate simply to help the "losing side," but
when he considers the prospect of a communal economic system

—which some of Sillitoe's later heroes are dedicated to establishing—
Arthur quickly recants. As he explains to Jack,

I've 'eard that blokes as win football pools get thousands o' beggin'
letters, but yer know what I'd do if I got 'em? I'll tell yer what I'd do:
I'd mek a bonfire on 'em. Because I don't believe in share and share
alike, Jack. Tek them blokes as spout on boxes outside the factory
sometimes. I like to hear 'em talk about Russia, about farms and
power-stations they've got, because it's interestin', but when they say
that when they get in government everybody's got to share and share
alike, then that's another thing. I ain't a communist, I tell you. (32)

This independence of spirit helps make Seaton a more dynamic
character than the hero of *The Death of William Posters* and *A Tree on
Fire,* Frank Dawley, who is less an individual than a man whose essence
is that he is dedicated to the cause of Communist revolution.

III *The Family of Man*

Saturday Night and Sunday Morning is far from being simply a social
thesis novel that presents the eternal conflict between labor and
management. Seaton's job and the anger which he exhibits toward the
"haves" are simply aspects of his existence, not his essence. Maloff
notes, "The 'action,' the motive, the force in Sillitoe's work which has
the power to transform is not the ethos of 'I'm all right, Jack,' nor is it
the black hatred which often seems the strongest emotion his characters
are capable of feeling. . . . The emotion, rather, is that of class
loyalty—it would not be excessive, indeed, to speak of class love; and
the general movement of feeling in Sillitoe's best and truest work
gravitates from isolation to affiliation, from nonidentity to identity,
from the sense of being man alone in the jungle . . . to the knowledge of
being man connected, related to others not only by the fact of sharing a
common predicament, but common joy and vitality as well." [7] This
aspect of Arthur's existence is best represented in his ties with his
family, which Sillitoe is capable of rendering with an intimacy
reminiscent of Charles Dickens's talent. A sense of security and
solidarity permeates one afternoon when Arthur and his father return
home to the living room where they join Vera (the mother), Margaret
(Arthur's sister), and Margaret's five-year-old son, William. Because
Sillitoe is careful to provide the details that make our familiarity with
his people convincing, we know the substance of their meals—"a special
pay-day treat of bacon-and-beans"—and the ritual of their habits:

"They never touched a bite until two cups of tea stood emptied by their unwashed hands." We see Arthur Seaton as something other than a lathe operator or young rake as he balances his nephew William on his knee and spins a tale:

"Now then, yer little bogger, let me tell yer a story." He accentuated his gruff voice. "Once upon a time—sit still then, or I wain't tell yer. Tek yer fingers out o' my tea—there was a bad man who lived in a dark wood, in a gret big castle, wi' water drippin' down the walls, and spider-webs as big as eiderdowns in every corner, winders that creaked and trapdoors everywhere that swallered people up if they made a false move. . . ." (62)

To William, whose own father is a drunkard and a wife beater, Seaton is a much-needed object of affection; William can throw his arms about him, "loving his rich uncle who came from the towering world of work and sent pound notes across the dazzling air of the Friday-night kitchen" (65). This picture of Arthur as father substitute foreshadows his acceptance, at the end of the novel, of the role of husband and father.

Arthur's philosophy in the world of men is based on "cunning," but, despite his sexual opportunism, he does not hold the same attitude toward women. He thinks of them as "creatures that needed and deserved to be looked after, requiring all the attention a man could give, certainly more than the man's work and a man's own pleasure" (41). In this novel, the relationship between man and woman holds the place of first importance; it is the oldest relationship and, Sillitoe suggests, perhaps the only enduring one between human beings. Arthur conveys this belief when he thinks, "The factory did not matter. The factory could go on working until it blew itself up from too much speed, but I, he thought, already a couple of dozen above his daily stint, will be here after the factory's gone, and so will Brenda and all women like her still be here, the sort of women that are worth their weight in gold" (42). The novel as a whole expresses a faith in the continuance of man, particularly of the common man. And, as we have already observed, this positive faith is balanced against much in Sillitoe's work that is merely a negative criticism of society.

Seaton's progress through the novel is an educative experience, growing out of the conflict between his love of independence and his dedication to the love of women. He is to learn that in becoming involved with humanity, he must accept not only the resultant pleasure but also the difficulties. When Brenda becomes pregnant, Arthur discovers to his surprise that she does not want to have another child, not because of the burden of pregnancy or the pain of childbirth, but because "you've got ter look after it every minute for fifteen years" (70). At this stage in the novel, the matter of responsibility is not altogether clear to Arthur, but he is beginning to sense the nature of the human predicament: that being part of the family of man necessarily involves pain. At the moment, "he could see no need of all this fuss, and understood once more why in these happy days men joined the army: to escape the smoke that came from other people's fires. People made too much fuss about useless things, but you have to get caught by it, or at least join in the chorus of their moans and groans, otherwise life would not go on and you would be left in some old doss-house, neglected like an apple-coking by everybody in the world" (73). Thus, Sillitoe begins early in the novel to develop the theme of his conclusion: "Whenever you caught a fish, the fish caught you" (236).

IV *The Cycle of Existence*

The first eight chapters of *Saturday Night and Sunday Morning* are devoted to Arthur's work at the factory, to his adultery with the sisters Brenda and Winnie, to Brenda's abortion, and to various drunken pranks which Arthur and his elder brother Fred play. The ninth chapter introduces a change in tone. Until this point in the novel, Arthur's mind has not carried itself into the future much beyond the cycle of work week, week end, to "grab like owt to earn a few quid, to take Brenda boozing and back to bed, or to the footpaths and woods up Strelley" (35). On the whole, his feeling about his existence has been one of equanimity; he believes that he has been having the "good life" and "couldn't care less if the world did blow up tomorrow" (37).

Such hybris is always in danger of being brought low in Sillitoe's works. Seaton senses the danger, and he is also bothered by the nagging thought that the illicit love which he has been enjoying, with its constant danger of discovery, compares unfavorably with a more stable union in which he could "live all the time with a woman . . . and sleep in a bed with her that belonged to both of you, that no one could turn you out of if they caught you there" (137). This tentative concern with the future turns his mind to the larger cycle of existence: "The future meant things, both good and bad, to look forward to, like the coming of summer (good), military training at the end of August (purgat'ry), Goose Fair in October (smashin'), Bonfire Night (good if you didn't get blown to bits), and Christmas at Christmas. Then the new year swung its fist and dragged you blindfolded and by the neck-scruff onto the high crest of another wave" (137).

In the ninth chapter, the season is summer, and Sillitoe begins preparing for the beginning of the end of Arthur's idyllic life as he portrays a scene which foreshadows the conclusion of the novel. On Sundays, Arthur escapes the repetitious "prison-like" existence of factory work by riding his bicycle four miles to the peace of the countryside. There he sits on a canal bank below Hemlock Stone and the Bramcote Hills, casting his fishing line into the still water. In the factory and in the city, time is measured primarily by clocks and calendars; for Arthur, time, as it is measured by the earth through the changing seasons, is recognizable only during moments of escape to the countryside. On one such trip, described in Chapter 9, Brenda points out the inevitable future for him: "Everybody thinks they'll never get married at your age. So did Jack, he told me. You think you can go on all your life being single, I remember he said, but you suddenly find out you can't" (144).

Hugh B. Staples, in his excellent study of the relationship of Robert Graves's *The White Goddess* to *Saturday Night and Sunday Morning,* describes the progress of Seaton's educative experience: "As the zodiac runs its course, Arthur is gradually, but progressively, made aware of the truth that actions have consequences, and that society will ultimately hold him responsible for them, wiggle and squirm as he may to avoid being held accountable. It is, in other words, the idea of responsibility that he is anxious above all to reject, but the symbolic figure of the White Goddess, as she is represented in the figures of Brenda, Aunt Ada and Doreen, functions to make sure that he does not escape his fate."[8] His fate, quite simply, is that he must experience a fall from his position as Lord of Misrule and accept Women—we need not style her a White Goddess—as a mate rather than as a concubine, which has in effect been Brenda's position. The adulterous relationship which ends in unnatural abortion must be supplanted by a union between Arthur and a young woman who can become his wife and the mother of his children.

During his two-week army summer training (also described in Chapter 9), Arthur is given an ominous warning as he returns from a drinking bout in a village near the camp. Ambling along complacently, hands in pockets and whistling a tune, he abruptly encounters "A lightning flash, purple and brilliant. . . . He saw trees grouped together that he had not noticed before. In the cannonade of thunder that followed his tune went unconsciously on, but the first flash ploughed a furrow through the depths of his mind into which entered the second broad wink of lightning. He felt afraid, and his legs began to tremble. 'What's up?' he said. Then louder: 'What's up?' He walked on in the dull even descent of the rain, counting each second between lightning and thunder. Then he resumed his whistling, a marching tune that kept him swinging along. . ." (148–49). What the thunder said is that the freedom of Arthur's youth is approaching its end, and the obligations of maturity lie in wait for him.

Returning to Nottingham and gladly exchanging the stiff military uniform for the comfort of his civilian clothes, he expects to return easily to the steady, pleasant existence of Brenda, pubs, fishing, and factory, that he has enjoyed before. He finds, however, that Brenda's affection for him has cooled, nominally because he had not written to her, and that her sister Winnie is now indifferent to him because she is sure that other men will make themselves available to her. Leaving the two sisters sitting in a pub, Seaton angrily indulges in a bit of self-righteous indignation that is superbly humorous because of his own past actions: "Never again. They'd had all they were going to get from him. Brenda wasn't worth the trouble he'd been through to keep her. . . . Most likely, when he went away, she had been glad to see the back of him, and had passed the whole fortnight doing the dirty on him, not to mention on poor old Jack. Instead of boozing in the Match she should be at home looking after her two kids, the poor little sods" (155).

More importantly, Seaton has begun to fashion in his mind the conditions which he deems necessary for a satisfactory marriage: "If ever I get married, he thought, and have a wife that carries on like Brenda and Winnie carry on, I'll give her the biggest pasting any woman ever had. I'd kill her. My wife'll have to look after any kids I fill her with, keep the house spotless. And if she's good at that I might let her go to the pictures now and again and take her out for a drink on Saturday" (155). He walks to another pub and, striking up a conversation with the lady tending bar, asserts loudly that he does not intend to get married. A moment later, he meets his future fiancée, Doreen Greatton, aged nineteen, attractive and inexperienced. Their courtship begins when he arranges to meet her at a local theater on the following night. Adjusting to the new relationship, Arthur likes not having to fear irate husbands, but he also realizes that he is heading toward "the dizzy and undesired brink of hell that older men called marriage" (166). Reluctantly, but inescapably, Arthur begins to submit to his fate.

V *The Fall of the King*

At the end of Part I of the novel, the autumn celebration of Goose Fair approaches. Traditionally, young men take their sweethearts to

the event; but, when Doreen hints for Arthur to take her on a Saturday
night, he makes one last vainglorious attempt to escape fate: he
arranges to escort both Brenda and Winnie to the fair on that night. The
fair is descirbed as a fantastic pulsating machine which devours
humanity. Approaching the fairgrounds, Arthur, Brenda, and Winnie
"heard the thumping pistons of red-painted engines that gave power to
caterpillars and Noah's Arks, and distant screams came down at them
from the tower of Helter Skelter and the topmost arc of the Big Wheel,
noise and lights a magnetized swamp sucking people into it for miles
around" (170). Placing the festival strategically near the end of the first
section of the novel (in Chapter 11), Sillitoe intensifies its significance
by suggesting its psychological effect upon the crowd: "Sanity was out
of reach: they were caught up in balloons of light and pleasure that
would not let them go. The four-acre fair became a whole world, with
tents and caravans, stalls and roundabouts, booths and towers,
swingboats and engines and big wheels, and a crowd that had lost all
idea of time and place, locked in the belly of its infernal noise" (172).

The fair is an appropriate setting for the inevitable end of Arthur
Seaton's chaotic, unrestrained youth. Riding on a Ghost Train which
assails its passengers with frightening darkness and horrible screams
from hell, Arthur stands up to fight the "mock-death whose horrors
had been written in large letters across the facade outside" (172). He
moves about from car to car, frightening various passengers; and at last
he undergoes a ludicrous but symbolic "death" himself. Reaching up
for a skeleton painted on a huge piece of cloth, he becomes entangled
and is "buried . . . six feet under in a sackcloth coffin" (174). Freeing
himself at last, he shouts out to the crowd, "I've won . . . I beat that
bloody skeleton!" His last moment of triumph comes when, high atop a
giant slide called the Helter Skelter, "He looked over the lights and tent
tops and people bellowing out a rough voice to the sky, at the three-day
ritual bout of forty thousand voices. He felt like a king up there with so
much power spreading on all sides below him . . ." (176). As he speeds
down the slide, however, he is besieged by a rush of thoughts and a
nagging question: "There was nothing to do but wait. . . . But wait for
what?" (176). He finds the answer at the bottom of the ride, for there
waiting for him are the two outraged husbands of the women whom he
has been squiring. Seaton manages to escape their wrath, but his escape
is only momentary.

Like a fugitive, he attempts to evade his punishment; but, as he
himself realizes, he is "caught in a game of fang-and-claw with a
dangerous hand of aces." Part I concludes with Arthur's being beaten

brutally by Winnie's husband and another soldier. The opening of Part II, "Sunday Morning," presents him in an apathetic state, hardly caring whether he lives or dies. His "nameless malady" arises, Sillitoe suggests, from a number of causes: he has lost the opportunity (Arthur calls it "the right") of loving two attractive women at once; the realization that he has been physically beaten "on the common battleground of the jungle"; and, most importantly, the notion that the two men who beat him "represented the raw edge of fang-and-claw on which all laws were based, law and order against which he had been fighting all his life in such a thoughtless unorganized way that he could not but lose" (194). The concept of the "jungle" is important, for it is repeatedly emphasized in Sillitoe's works and implies a negation of all concepts of social order.

In Seaton's case, however, the notion of life as nothing other than a "jungle" is less a fact of existence than a state of mind. Seaton has had only one beating; in his mental exaggeration of that experience, he comes to believe that man's existence is without sanctuary: "he knew for the first time in his life that there had never been any such thing as safety, and never would be, the difference being that now he knew it as a fact, whereas before it was a natural unconscious state. If you lived in the middle of a dark wood you weren't safe, not by a long way, he thought, and you had to sleep always with one eye open and a pile of sharp stones by your side, within easy reach of your fist" (197). The philosophy is primitivistic and would perhaps be a workable philosophy for a man who lives in isolation—"in the middle of a dark wood"—but the man who abides by it must isolate himself from the rest of humanity, which Seaton has no intention of doing. Knowing that Jack is probably partly responsible for the beating which he has received, Arthur momentarily considers striking back, extracting "an eye for an eye and a tooth for a tooth," but, upon further reflection, he concludes that it is not worth it and that he has had "more than his fair share" of such an existence.

VI *A New Life*

Part II presents a Christmas interlude involving the family of Arthur's Aunt Ada, who, at age fifty, "still had the personality of a promiscuous barmaid, a kindness to listen to any man's tale and sob like a twin-soul into his beer, even to bring him home to bed if she thought it would make him feel better" (77). By her first husband, Doddoe, she had borne eleven children; her second husband, Ralph, had

brought from an earlier marriage five more children to the household,
which creates a sense of happy familial chaos in the Christmas scene at
their home. The gathering is further enlarged by Sam, a Gold Coast
Negro who had made friends with Johnny, one of the Doddoe boys,
and had been invited to visit during the holidays. The mood of the
sequence is one of happy confusion: there are scrapes in public houses,
jocular and bantering conversation, tales of derring-do by the outlaw
Doddoe clan—and, finally, tables of food and bumpers of ale consumed
in the warm kitchen atmosphere.

The experience provides the proper catalyst to bring Arthur out of
the torpor that has characterized his mind and spirit since the beating at
the hands of the soldiers. His transformation is finally effected when
one of the Doddoe girls, Jane, breaks a drinking glass on the head of her
surprised husband, Jim, who in his confusion can only exclaim, "Why
did you hit me? . . . What did I say? . . . Tell me, somebody, what did I
say?" (219). No explanation is given, nor, apparently, is one needed;
the vitality of this martial violence speaks of life and is in itself enough
to return Seaton to the fray of existence: "now he was awake once
more, ready to tackle all obstacles, to break any man, or woman, that
came for him, to turn on the whole world if it bothered him too much,
and blow it to pieces. The crack of the glass on Jim's forehead echoed
and re-echoed through his mind" (219).

The return of Seaton's vitality also restores his rebellious spirit.
Following the Christmas celebration, his thoughts turn angrily to
"factories and labour exchanges and insurance offices" which,
respectively, "sweat you to death . . . talk you to death . . . and rob you
to death" (220). His rebellion is, as before, generously self-pitying, and
he repeats his earlier sentiment: "Ay, by God, it's a hard life if you
don't weaken" (220). It may be difficult for the reader to conceive
how Seaton, who has a "good hundred pounds worth" of dress-clothing
in his closet and enough cash to keep his life filled with ale and women,
can justify his self-pity.

The explanation seems to be that, like Dostoevsky's "Underground
Man," what most arouses Seaton's rebellion is the assumption by those
in high places that his wants and needs are quite predictable, that his
will and his value as an individual count for next to nothing. He turns
his wrath upon the most obvious targets—the government, labor
officials, the police, the wealthy:

One day they'll flash their lamps and clap their hands and say: "Come
on, lads. Line up and get your money. We won't let you starve." But
some of us will want to starve, and that'll be where the trouble'll start.

Perhaps some'll want to play football, or go fishing up Grantham Cut. . . . Blokes with suits and howler hats will say: "These chaps have got their television sets, enough to live on, council houses, beer and pools—some have even got cars. We've made them happy. What's wrong?" (221)

Unlike Dostoevsky's paradoxical character, however, Seaton cannot be satisfied by simply going "underground." He singles out "cunning" as the only effective weapon, but he specifically rejects "quiet cunning— which was worse than being dead" and favors instead "the broad-fisted exuberant cunning of a man who worked all day in a factory" (222). The practical effect of all of his thought about rebellion is that it brings him to the realization that he can safely maintain his rebellious spirit and at the same time accept some of "The sweet and agreeable things of life," but with less difficulty than he encountered in pursuing them with Brenda and Winnie.

Seaton's courtship with Doreen is continued in the month of March, as Sillitoe presents another idyllic country scene. Arthur has known since his youth the countryside along a path leading to Ilkeston, and it recalls to him the independent days which he had spent at his grandfather's, a blacksmith who had his forge and home in Wollaton village: "you had drawn your own water from a well, dug your own potatoes out of the garden, taken eggs from the chicken run to fry with bacon off your own side of pig hanging salted from a hook in the pantry" (223). Those days, he recognizes, are gone, and there is no returning, nor is there an escape into nature for Seaton and Doreen away from the "fang-like claws" of the world. In a sensitively rendered passage, Sillitoe describes a moment of recognition which occurs when the two are standing beside a stream:

White and blue sky made islands on it, so that the descent into its hollows seemed deep and fathomless, and fishes swam over enormous gulfs and chasms of cobalt blue. Arthur's eyes were fixed into the beautiful earth-bowl of the depthless water, trying to explore each pool and shallow until, as well as an external silence there was a silence within himself that no particle of his mind or body wanted to break. Their faces could not be seen in the water, but were united with the shadows of the fish that flitted among upright reeds and spreading lilies, drawn to the water as if they belonged there, as if the fang-like claws of the world would come unstuck from their flesh if they descended into its imaginary depths, as if they had known it before as a refuge and wanted to return to it, their ghosts already there, treading the calm unfurrowed depths and beckoning them to follow.

But there was no question of following. You were dragged down sooner or later whether you liked it or not. A ripple appeared in the middle of the water, expanded in concentric rings, and burst by a timeless force of power. (225)

There is no escape into tranquillity, because life is struggle, as is love. Soon after their interlude beside the stream, Seaton and Doreen begin to fall into a pattern of argument and reconciliation which makes them feel as if they were already married. Arthur does not regard their amorous strife as a forewarning but as a healthy and inevitable part of their relationship.

In the last chapter of the novel, following Arthur's proposal, Sillitoe makes his final thematic point through a metaphor of angling. Arthur began the novel fiercely independent at the age of twenty-one, tumbling down the steps of the White-Horse public house dead drunk on a Saturday night; he ends it at the age of twenty-four engaged to be married and fishing tranquilly by the side of a quiet stream. Reflecting upon what seems to him to be the human situation, he concludes that the notion of absolute freedom and independence is not only untenable but undesirable:

"Whenever you caught a fish, the fish caught you, in a way of speaking, and it was the same with anything else you caught, like the measles or a woman. Everyone in the world was caught, somehow, one way or another, and those that weren't were always on the way to it. As soon as you were born you were captured by fresh air that you screamed against the minute you came out. . . . Mostly you were like a fish: you swam about with freedom, thinking how good it was to be left alone, doing anything you wanted to do and caring about no one, when suddenly: SPLUTCH!—the big hook clapped itself into your mouth and you were caught." (236)

Although he realizes that he is not caught yet—that he can break the engagement and escape from Doreen—he does not want to do so, for such independence at last excludes one from meaningful life: "If you went through life refusing all the bait dangled before you, that would be no life at all. No changes would be made and you would have nothing to fight against. Life would be as dull as ditchwater" (236).

The same man who concluded earlier in the novel that "cunning" was the only reliable tool of man, now concedes, "You could kill yourself by too much cunning" (236). Seaton lands a fish, recognizes its kinship with him, and then, in a symbolic gesture, releases it after looking into its eyes, which mirror "the memory of cunning curves executed in the moving shadows from reed to reed." It is a brief truce in the struggle that constitutes life, but Seaton recognizes that such tranquillity can not make up his own existence: "There's bound to be trouble in store for me every day of my life, because trouble it's always been and always will be," but his conclusion is optimistic: "it's a good life and a good world, all said and done, if you don't weaken, and if you know that the big wide world hasn't heard from you yet, no, not by a long way, though it won't be long now" (239). This optimistic acceptance of life is continued, as we shall see, in *Key to the Door,* but there it undergoes some important modifications.

VII *Critical Reception*

The reaction to *Saturday Night and Sunday Morning* was, on the whole, favorable. Those who found the work undeserving of the general praise which it received usually based their objections upon the morality of the hero rather than upon the artistic merit of the work. Frederick R. Karl, for example, complained that *"Saturday Night and Sunday Morning* (1958) was praised by the press as the best proletarian novel since the thirties. Actually, the novel is less than that, although it is effective on a small scale and in a minor key. Sillitoe's Arthur Seaton is an angry young worker, a 'heel,' who, on weekends, escapes from his factory job by going on drunken sprees. The cataloguing of Seaton's picaresque adventures forms the spine of the novel, as he goes with great vitality from drink to the female-cushioned bed, and then returns to drink."[9] Similarly, Paul Crane contended, "Alan Sillitoe's hero is shallow. He is shrewd, certainly, but there is no depth to his character. Yet a man needs depth to feel frustration and react against it. Moreover, in the context of the gregarious instincts of his class, Arthur Seaton's amoral opportunism is much better understood in terms of a pathetic desire to be one of the crowd than to stand away from it."[10]

Most critics, however, felt that Sillitoe's first novel signaled the beginning of a brilliant career. As we have noted earlier, Anthony West felt that by writing *Saturday Night and Sunday Morning* Sillitoe had "assured himself a place in the history of the English novel"; Malcolm Bradbury was persuaded by the work that "Mr. Sillitoe is one of the best English writers of the day."[11] Sillitoe's realism accounted for much of the praise; readers could sense that Sillitoe's empathy with workingmen's attitudes and his detailed familiarity with their environment came from knowledge acquired firsthand. John Dennis Hurrell's remark is typical: "others have given us novels of provencial working-class life. But nobody has given us such absolute verisimilitude."[12]

We expect a novel like *Saturday Night and Sunday Morning* to be praised for its realism, but perhaps even more indicative of the critical response to the work is a study like that of Hugh B. Staples, who saw in the novel mythic significance echoing Robert Graves's *The White Goddess* and T. S. Eliot's *The Waste Land:* "For although a great deal in the novel may be taken as both implicit and explicit proletarian criticism of the Establishment and its works, the central idea is deeper and more nearly universal: it is a dramatic analysis, on an essentially comic level, of the immemorial rhythms of birth, life and death that Robert Graves maintains is the theme of 'all true poets' from Homer to the present day."[13]

Those reviewers who expressed doubts and reservations were usually less concerned with the merit of *Saturday Night and Sunday Morning* than with Sillitoe's future as an author. Such reviewers warned that the first novel might have been successful because it was youthful autobiography, a type of achievement not easily repeated. They warned too, that working-class life might prove to be too limited in its significance to merit extensive literary treatment. Whatever the virtue of those arguments, it is evident that none of Sillitoe's subsequent novels has generated the critical enthusiasm accorded *Saturday Night and Sunday Morning.* Precisely why this is so will be explored in the following chapters.

CHAPTER 6

The General

I *Critical Reception*

IF the expectations aroused by Sillitoe's first novel were somewhat too optimistic, the reaction to his second novel, *The General*, was excessively pessimistic. Several circumstances were prejudicial to a favorable reception of the work. For one thing, reviewers are not immune from the human frailty of exaggerating the potentiality of a new writer and then undervaluing his worth when his name has become more familiar. For another, *The General* was not the type of material expected of a writer who in his first two books seemed appropriately classified as a chronicler of English lower-class life: the work is not set in Nottingham; it is not interwoven with class conflict and social protest; and it contains no characters speaking the dialects and argot which Sillitoe represents so well. Thus, Walter Allen registered his disapproval by concluding his *New Statesman* review with the injunction, "Back to your factory-hands and Borstal boys, Mr. Sillitoe!" [1] Finally, it seemed to some critics that Sillitoe might have written the work hurriedly in order to capitalize on the successes of *Saturday Night and Sunday Morning* and *The Loneliness of the Long-distance Runner.* *The General* was, after all, the third volume of fiction published by Sillitoe in as many years. The fact is, however, that the work actually began as a short story composed in Nottingham in 1949 and was later developed into a novel while the author was living in Majorca in 1953. Seven years later, after subsequent revisions in Soller and Hertfordshire, Sillitoe released *The General* for publication. [2]

Aside from these considerations, some reviewers apparently did not grasp that the work was intended to be a fable. The reviewer in the *Times Literary Supplement,* for example, while recognizing that the work was not intended to be realistic, attacked it for its lack of realism, stating that Sillitoe had produced "a fantasy, built upon a mixture of improbabilities and impossibilities. He creates a world very different from the world we know and puts it in a state of war utterly unlike any war we are ever likely to be involved in."[3] He objects to the fact that the soldiers represented in the novel do not have airplanes, that they have primitive units called "knife troops," that they take no prisoners, that their officers sometimes kill their own troops, that some of the men practice cannibalism, and that a railroad "train is stopped—by a horseman!"

To attack the novel upon such grounds is, of course, to miss its point. Sillitoe's accomplishments in realistic fiction are sufficient to assure the reader that the author knows the difference between that type of writing and the fable. As the *Times* review illustrates, the author cannot always be sure that his readers will be able to make the same distinctions. Admittedly, *The General* is quite distinct from Sillitoe's other works, in much the same way that *A Fable* is an anomaly in William Faulkner's canon, and that difference may explain some of the confusion; but to evaluate such works in terms of realistic criteria is to grossly misread them. Faulkner made such an error virtually impossible by clearly labeling the contents of his work; Sillitoe may regret not having done likewise. It would be inaccurate and unfair to imply that the novel was everywhere misunderstood. Max Cosman produced an excellent, perceptive short review of the work; and Gouverneur Paulding and Walter Allen certainly did not fail to observe that the novel was intended to be symbolic.[4] However, *The General* has not been widely appreciated or understood.

II *Man, the Aggressive Animal*

The structural organization of the work is not complex. Following a plotting device dating from the novels of Samuel Richardson, Sillitoe establishes early in the novel a circumstance which might appropriately be described as sustained deadlock. The formula calls for a captivity from which there is no feasible escape; a psychological confrontation between an antagonistic captor and his captive; and, at the end of the novel, a release from captivity and, possibly, the resolution of some philosophical, social, or personal conflict. In *The General,* ninety-five noncombatant personnel, all members of a symphony orchestra, are being taken to the front lines by train to entertain the forces of their country; but, before they reach their destination, they are taken captive by enemy troops, the Gorsheks. While the orchestra is held captive for several days in a barn, the orchestra leader—Evart—and the commander of the Gorshek forces—known only as the General—debate their opposing views of man, art, and war. The General, torn by conflicting loyalties, at last releases his prisoners, thereby disobeying the commands of his superiors. As the novel concludes, the orchestra is returning to its own lines, presumably to safety; the General is a captive of his own military forces as a result of his humanitarian gesture.

As the outline suggests, Sillitoe has written a "novel of ideas," and it has the usual shortcomings of that type. There is little of the intense verisimilitude that we find in his depictions of workers, thieves, and outcasts in his novels and short stories set in Nottingham; and there is perhaps too much philosophical dialogue and too little action, but the ideas presented deserve consideration. The novel, as a fable, examines the nature of man. To direct our attention to the subject, Sillitoe has—no doubt deliberately—introduced anachronisms, a point which disturbed the *Times* reviewer: there are trains and electronic computers but no airplanes or hydrogen bombs. The reason for such a novelistic "error" is not difficult to discover; the author is suggesting, quite simply, that man's difficulties have less to do with his technology than with his nature.

What man's nature appears to be, on the surface, is conveyed in the opening scene in which two violinists—men dedicated by profession but not by nature to harmony—are seen quarreling over the possession of a single packet of sugar with which each intends to sweeten his tea. The incident suggests that man is petty and irascible by nature, but he is not simply that. He can also be incredibly brutal, as when, a few pages later, the rabble Gorshek troops prepare to slaughter the orchestra members for their instruments and personal possessions, but are instead slaughtered by one of their own officers, Kondal, who cares more for discipline than for human life.

Behind these instances of pettiness and of individual cruelty is a background of man's larger destructive capabilities—his propensity for organizing societies which propagate war. Sillitoe avoids the simplistic explanations which some of his other writings might lead us to expect from him, for he does not attribute national conflicts to the machinations of a few corrupt leaders hungry for power and wealth. Nor does he turn to the expediency of quasi-Marxist propaganda, as he later did in the final sections of *Key to the Door* and throughout most of *A Tree on Fire,* by depicting a ragged "army of liberation" struggling heroically against a well-equipped capitalist force.

His purpose is to probe the cause of war, not to propagandize for one ideology or another. There are general differences between the two warring civilizations: the Gorsheks are on the whole more barbaric, their opponents more cultured; but, as Evart concludes, there is "very little difference between that civilization, and this 'method of life' that our side are so busy fighting" (149). The causes of war lie within the diverse capabilties of the human spirit, which are represented in this novel primarily in the characterizations of the orchestra leader and the General.

III *The Pacifist and the Warrior*

Evart, who is humanitarian, selfless, pacifistic, and politically neutral, represents a civilizing force contained, presumably, in every man. His attitude toward the armed barbarism in which the Gorsheks and his country are engaged is unequivocal: "I don't believe in war, no matter what problems have to be solved. Problems that have to be solved by war aren't legitimate problems at all" (66). The most frequently proffered justification of war—freedom—has in too many cases been synonymous with tyranny, he contends. Such freedom as man is capable of attaining has less to do with release from physical bondage than with liberation from the destructive forces within himself, a liberation effected in no small degree by the restorative powers of man's art, especially by his music. Thus, the emotion which Evart experiences when faced by the menacing Gorsheks is not simply personal; he comes to know a fear "deeper than that of death: he stood before enemies that were greater than enemies who could merely kill you; by killing you they destroyed that which you had spent your life trying to represent and propagate" (30).

What Evart most fears is the general death of the creative will within man, He recognizes the destructive element within his own soul but does not fear it: "The Gorsheks are overrunning the earth with their barbarisms, and I've come to realize in the last few days that they're like something hidden in my own nature, something that's quiescent though, that I hardly need to fight. If it stopped being quiescent I should fight it, because if I didn't I'd be one of these people" (64). Evart thus represents a fixed point of view: he wages no internal battles and does not desire at any point in the novel to exchange his culture and pacifism for a more barbaric response to life. The dramatic intensity of the work, consequently, resides in the character of the General and in the implications of the work as a whole concerning man's fate.

In contrast to Evart, the General is a man capable of assimilating diverse and conflicting attributes. He resorts to expediencies unusually cruel, even for a professional military man; in one instance, he covertly supplies the advance guard of an assault force with explosive rations packets in order to insure that the rear troops will be signaled at precisely the right moment. Initially, war is to him (as music is to Evart) the quintessence of man's artistry. He considers armed conflict inevitable because of man's nature: "War is and always has been mainly an expression of timeless atavism . . . the boils in man's nature feeling the occasional necessity of suppuration" (66). And again, "It is also nature's way of filling the empty sack-bag of men's ideals; it puts a machine-gun into their hands when a theory has been pushed to the limits of their intelligence" (64).

The cynical and primitivistic philosophy which the General espouses is not a new element in Sillitoe's works. Where Smith of "The Loneliness of the Long-distance Runner" was firmly persuaded that "Cunning is what counts in life . . . " (7), the General simply expresses the conviction in collective rather than in individual terms: "You can put all the theories of the world into the earth and blow them up with dynamite, but one thing will still be there: power, the power of one nation over another, the simple dog-eat-dog of nation against nation fighting for what they call freedom. We call it survival" (65). If the General were capable of maintaining and following such a philosophy, the dénouement of the novel would be a simple, tragic one. The General would obey the orders of the High Command and, without remorse of conscience, put the orchestra to death at once.

His refusal to do so gives rise to the central philosophic questions of the novel: the nature of human freedom, the will of an organization versus that of an individual, and the conflict between man's destructive and creative impulses. Overshadowing these questions is a view of fate which is apparent in all of Sillitoe's works, a *Weltanschauung* which is both classic and tragic—man struggles, but his only victory may be the knowledge that he has not accepted defeat passively. The High Command is in a very real sense a symbol of the fate of modern man, his collective obedience to the organization will. This will is, as in Classical Greek tragedy, that which man cannot by wisdom or guile escape.

Man's struggle to escape is portrayed in the dilemma which the General faces in attempting to pit a somewhat crippled innate individualism against a learned obedience to duty. His predicament is not simply that of a professional military man but that of anyone who works in or is subject to a highly centralized and stratified organization. The conflict is similar to that presented in "The Loneliness of the

Long-distance Runner," but there are important differences. The long-distance runner, Smith, experienced little of the internal conflict which plagues the General. Smith was held captive by a system which he had long despised—the Borstals of respectable "In-law" society. His incarceration simply served to intensify the rebellious assertion of his individuality.

The General, in contrast, has a vested interest in the system to which he is subject; his position within the structure is at the top, not at the bottom, as was Smith's. By a small inconvenience to conscience—obeying orders rather than his personal convictions—he stands to do away with a potential threat to his career. By disobeying orders, he stands to lose a position of esteem and power and to face the degradation of being "levelled," the High Command's term for the combined humiliations of demotion, exile, and imprisonment. The General reflects on the consequences: "Levelled with what? he wondered. Levelled, he gathered, with the animals of the earth, chained out in the wilderness at the mercy of infinitely fickle seasons; heat, cold, starvation, and the whiplash of enforced labour" (84). In the face of such punishment, it is not difficult for the General, or any man, to muster arguments supporting obedience to duty. He considers various rationalizations: the inevitable abnegation of human will—"The Gorshek High Command have given the order to me. I can do nothing about it. There's nothing else to say or discuss, because their decision is final" (99); the brevity of guilt—"The death of his conscience would pass unnoticed in the intense paper-work necessary for preparing the spring offensive" (145); and the relative importance of his life weighed against that of the orchestra—"he considered himself more valuable to the Gorshek nation than a symphony orchestra was to the world" (170).

As comforting as these rationalizations may be, they do not, the General conceives, face directly the question of his ability to act as an individual according to his will. It seems to him that conscience has ultimately become in him a powerless attribute capable of commenting upon but not of directing his actions: "Freedom. The freedom to attain your own successes within a formulated pattern. The freedom to serve. The freedom to submit certain questions to those in authority above you. Your conscience was a god who stated but did not decide" (75). When at last he rejects his former pattern of existence to the extent of believing that he may, if he chooses, act contrary to the dictates of the High Command, he conceives, like Dostoevsky's Grand Inquisitor, that self-determination is less man's blessing than his curse: "Complete freedom, he thought, would be unutterable pain. I've the opportunity of making a momentous decision, which is as much freedom as I can bear" (173).

He is at last brought to his decision by the force of several considerations. First of all, he has grown to detest the High Command's electronic computers (reminiscent of Orwell's *1984*), programmed with official state policy so that they can respond instantaneously to questions such as the General's regarding the appropriate treatment for a captured orchestra. The answer is simple and direct: they are to be shot immediately; for prisoners of whatever description, even noncombatant musicians, cost "food, time, labour, and anxiety to guard" (99). Also influencing his decision is the orchestra's poignant rendering of Tchaikovsky's Symphony, No. 6 the *Pathétique,* which awakens in him long-forgotten impulses and causes him to see the "artistry of war" in a truer light:

tree stumps and mounds of rubble, horizontal levels of burning ground, spot heights covered by the representative fractions of dismembered bodies, streams red with blood an hour after sunrise, lanes of fire and roads of smoke, scorched hachuring to mark the heightened elevation of his searching guns. Only blood and the ploughing of bombardment kept the land from becoming desert, was all the justification he could find. The music illuminated his vision, and its final symphonic beats synchronized his resignation to the slow steps of advancing fate. (127)

For once, then, the creative, humanitarian forces within man subdue his primitive, destructive inclinations; but the final reading of Sillitoe's fable cannot be patently optimistic.

IV *"Our Hopeful Suffering"*

The General, having regained his freedom of choice by following his conscience rather than the orders of the High Command, loses his liberty to those who believe only in the efficacy of force. The orchestra members, having gained their freedom and their lives, do so only by acquiescing to the conditions which the General establishes for their release: they must arm themselves with rifles. When the pacifist Evart, after protesting that weapons are unnecessary, accedes to the conditions, he remarks that the General has "won"; Sillitoe then describes the orchestra leader shouldering "the unaccustomed burden of a loaded rifle, and another familiar burden to which he could as yet give no name" (182).

This burden, quite simply, is man's fate, which is to say, man's nature. The point is enforced shortly before the prisoners are released when the author inserts a brief episode to remind the reader of a similar scene at the beginning of the novel. Evart's reflections upon the homogeneity of man, of whatever race or culture, are disturbed by the sounds of several musicians arguing over which should be the first to wash himself at a bucket of water. When the argument degenerates into a scuffle, the bucket tips over, and the men stare at the spreading water "in silence, like children who had broken a precious toy" (149). The only tenable view of man's fate, the novel implies, is that which the General at last accepts: "We've no power to alter the circumstances that are unknowingly shaping our lives. We can only wait, in our happy oblivion, or hopeful suffering, for the results of these unknown movements to affect us" (187).

Such a conclusion leaves us with an impression of Sillitoe's view of man as a creature whose only assured victory lies in the knowledge that he has not passively accepted defeat. In most of his writings, including those novels discussed in the following chapters, Sillitoe has established himself as a writer of protest, advocating an equalitarian society and espousing distrust of management, the rich, the clergy, and intellectuals; but, as *The General* illustrates, there is also a dominant philosophical strain in his works far removed from the proletarian "New Left" writings of the 1950's, with which Sillitoe's works have usually been identified.

CHAPTER 7

Key to the Door

IN response to my questions about the composition of his third novel, Mr. Sillitoe wrote to me that "*Key to the Door* was in fact an amalgamation of two early novels, very much rewritten, with a third section (Ropewalk) added. The childhood section was written first in 1950, and the Malayan section in 1949. They were consistently rewritten and altered however up to the date of publication in 1961." [1] The extensive revision and the extended period of composition produced an uneven work, but it does contain some of Sillitoe's finest writing. As Frederick P. W. McDowell has observed, "The authentic realism of *Key to the Door* is its most immediately impressive aspect—the sure rendering of life in depression and war-time Nottingham and in cold-war Malaya. Sillitoe evokes with the precision of one who is saturated with his materials, their sights and sounds and smells." [2] In addition to its sensory realism, the novel is notable for its organization.

I *Structure*

The work is divided into four sections: "Prologue," "Nimrod," "The Ropewalk," and "The Jungle." The first two present the youth of Brian Seaton, the older brother of Arthur of *Saturday Night and Sunday Morning.* The last two sections are primarily concerned with Brian's young manhood in Nottingham and with his experiences as a British soldier in Malaya during the third year following the end of World War II. Sillitoe has carefully structured the novel with regard to setting and chronology. There are really two major segments in the novel: the first is composed of "Prologue" and "Nimrod"; the second, of "The Ropewalk" and "The Jungle." Both segments focus upon two major settings: the chapters in "Prologue" and "Nimrod" alternate between Nottingham, where Brian lives with his parents, and a small country home near Nottingham known as "the Nook," where Brian visits his maternal grandparents. The chapters in "The Ropewalk" and "The Jungle" alternate between Malaya and Nottingham. By shifting between two settings in the first half of the novel, Sillitoe gives his readers a clear impresson of the environments which have the greatest influence upon the formation of Brian's character: the hard urban life of Nottingham during the depression and the more secure and idyllic setting of the grandparents' farm. The urban existence predominates, however; of the fifteen chapters in the "Prologue" and "Nimrod" sections, nine are devoted to Nottingham and only four to the Nook. The last two chapters are split between the two locations.

In the second half of the novel, the alternations in setting between chapters are somewhat more complex in that they involve changes in time as well as place. In all of the chapters set in Malaya in "The Ropewalk," Brian is in his nineteenth year; in the Malaya chapters in "The Jungle" section, he is in his twentieth year. The Nottingham chapters in both sections turn back in time to present Brian's gradual development from ages fifteen to eighteen. The regular chronological progression of the Malaya chapters produces the usual effect of novelistic continuity: we see Brian develop with a new environment which we gradually come to understand. In the Nottingham chapters, the shift back in time and the movement forward to the moment of Brian's departure for Malaya gradually clarify the reasons behind the abrupt transformation of his character from the rather innocent and passive boy that he is at the end of "Nimrod" to the cynical and rebellious young man that he has become by the beginning of "The Ropewalk." The structuring device also serves to reinforce the fact that Brian's past is inseparable from his present. While he is in Malaya, his thoughts repeatedly turn back to Nottingham; for his experiences there have largely determined what he has become.

II *"Prologue"*

The world of Seaton's youth is England during the depression of the 1930's, an environment which Sillitoe effectively re-creates through the private dreams, anxieties, affection, and anguish of the Seaton family. In the opening pages of "The Prologue," Brian's mother, Vera, takes her son to a wading pool in order to escape the "bug-eaten back-to-backs" of the tenements in Albion Yard where they swell. Brian plays a child's game of clasping his hands over his ears in order to dull the shouts of other slum children and thereby to allow his imagination to escape to a "distant eldorado," a sun-filled storybook land where happier children play. As the boy wades, his mother's thoughts turn to the early experiences of her marriage: the escapes from leaking houses flooded with rain water and the moves to dry but flea-infested houses. Her memories are of the dole office and of brutality at the hands of her husband, Harold.

Sillitoe also imprints the environment indelibly upon the reader's mind through Brian's recollection of scenes from the past: his mother holding her head over a bucket to catch the dripping blood from a wound inflicted by Harold; his father sitting upon a stone floor littering the house with cockroaches smashed with a hammer; and himself riding high atop a furniture-laden hand cart as his parents move by moonlight from one slum dwelling to another to escape rent collectors. The relationships within the family alternate between tender affection and violent hostility. Arguments arise quickly, irrationally; sometimes they seethe beneath the surface for days.

The family's difficulties arise not only from their poverty but from Harold's violent nature and from his refusal to yield to anything. Warned by Vera that God would "pay him out," he shouts with a sneer, "What bastard God? . . . There ain't no bastard God" (44). When he is angered beyond his powers of expression, he catches hold of a table rim and sends it spinning across the room with pots and dishes rattling in every direction. The whole circumstance conveys a sense of the characters' being trapped—by ignorance, poverty, and godlessness—with no means of escape, or hope, in view.

III *"Nimrod"*

Having established in the "Prologue" the family life of Harold and Vera, Sillitoe turns in the second section, "Nimrod," to the early life of Brian. The Nook, the rural residence of Vera's parents, becomes a second home for Brian; and Sillitoe evokes nostalgically a past era by describing the gramophone playing "Nellie Gray" and the oil lamps lighting the kitchen. For Brian, the Nook holds memories of summer storms, dinners of thrush puddings, and walks with his grandfather through cornfields and meadows.

The title of the section is taken from grandfather Merton's affectionate name for Brian, Nimrod ("the mighty hunter before the Lord" described in Genesis); but neither Merton nor Sillitoe is inclined to place faith in religion. Parodying the Flood, Sillitoe portrays a deluge with thunder and lightning which frightens the young huntsman Brian but which provides a diversion for his grandfather Merton. Disdaining the warning of his wife that the mere act of having steel utensils on the table during a storm is inviting retribution from God, the old blacksmith grasps a handful of knives and forks and holds them outside the window in defiance. When a "sheet of blue light" covers the window, Brian is convinced that his grandfather has been struck down; but Merton, unscathed, flings the cutlery on the table "contemptuous at its inability to kill him" (57). Religion is for Sillitoe little more than man's inclination to react to the inexplicable with fear. Mrs. Merton (Mary) is the prototype of Sillitoe's believer: "she did everything as if God were watching her: never threw bread on the fire (which was feeding the devil), never ill-treated a dumb animal, never turned a beggar away from the door. Even forty years with Merton had kept these principles alive, and they were so strongly instilled into her eight children that their children would also live by them" (58). Much more wholesome, from Sillitoe's point of view, is Merton's inclination to consider religion as a delightful folk tale. When asked by Brian what makes lightning and thunder, he explains that God sent Saint Paul to get a load of coal from hell; and, when Paul dumped the coal, it made a thunderous noise; lightning, in turn, is produced by the opening of the furnaces in hell.

Throughout the second section of the novel, Sillitoe carefully alternates the setting between the farm and the city. After the security and quiet isolation of the Nook, he turns to a sprawling city dump, littered with the refuse of months of "tipping" by trucks that haul the scrap from industrial Nottingham. Through shavings of aluminum, steel, and brass and amid smells of carbolic acid, oil, and rotting lumber, Brian searches with other boys and men for salable objects. Like the circles of Dante's *Inferno,* the scene vividly suggests chaos and decay, but it does so in terms suitable to the novel's setting. There are "half-submerged bedticks and 'steads, spokeless bicycle wheels without tyres sticking like rising suns out of black oily water, old boxes rotting away, a dinted uninhabited bird cage in front like a buoy at sea. Farther in the canal direction lay a dog-carcass sprawled half out of the water, its scabby grey pelt smoothed down by wind and rain" (73).

The huge building in which the refuse is incinerated suggests a modern inferno. Brian climbs inside a window of the deserted building and views the idle ovens and mounds of trash which are to be burned when the building opens again. He sees "mountains of dustbin rubbish ready for burning after the weekend, tins and boxes and cinders stretching in waves away from the wall to form an escarpment at the dozen doors of the cooling stoves. . . . The oven-doors had been bolted and shutter-drawn; they looked harmless, not like monsters' mouths any more but corpse-grey and a bit ghostly, sinister in their temporary inaction" (78).

The silent building—lighted by rays of sun streaming through the high arched windows—seems to Brian like "the inside of a church." Such apparent incongruity is not gratuitous in Sillitoe, for he tends to see beauty in those environs and circumstances from which he, like Brian, sprang, whatever the world may think of them. In his long poem "The Rats," he observed, "The wasteland that seemed to Mr. Eliot death/Nurtured me with passion, life and breath" (44). The sanitation department building, the author suggests, is as much of God, heaven, or church as Brian is ever likely to know, just as a spiritual "wasteland" is the heritage of the modern age.

The few ideas which Brian has of divinity are mostly associated with retributive justice. When he discovers that his cousin Bert has stolen the prized possession—a brass-handled rake—from one of the poor men at the dump and that Bert has himself lost the rake in the trash of the building, Brian wrestles with the confused notions of divinity which his parents have given him. Since Bert has lost the rake, it seems to Brian that his mother's conception of God dispensing justice to the wicked is a valid one: "God paid him out for nicking Agger's best rake." But when he reflects that the man who owned the rake will not have it restored to him, he recalls the sentiments of his father: "There ain't no God. God is a bastard . . ." (81).

Unable to resolve the conflicting notions of divinity, Brian turns to the only emotion left him: sympathy for the man who has been robbed. "I'm sorry for Agger, though, I am. I'm sorry for 'im. Out o' wok and living off the tips. I don't know. Nowt but an overcoat and an old pram to his name; and not even his posh rake anymore. I'm fed up, I am. God-all-bleedin'-mighty, I'm fed up" (82). The author, however, through an overview which concludes the scene, provides his own comment on the nature of God, indicating that man is, as Thomas Hardy phrased it, "God-Forgotten": "Westwards the sky had reddened, as if a nightwatchman behind the clouds had lit his fire for the night, sitting there to keep out intruders from what paradise lay beyond . . ." (82). If the metaphor is taken literally, man presumably has as little hope of escaping his suffering and entering paradise as did the sinners in Dante's *Inferno*.

Visits to the trash dump form only one important part of Brian's educative experience. Sillitoe brings home with force and clarity the difficulty of Brian's struggle to rise above the illiteracy which binds his father. The culture which is most available to him is that portrayed in gangster films, in the pornographic illustrated "Book of Nature" which his older friend Dave Doddoe reads, and in comic books which convey "grandiose ideas of destruction" (146). These media are designed to lead his mind to an intellectual cul-de-sac; for Brian to escape involves a greater struggle than most might imagine.

The first obstacle, not surprisingly, is economic, the other, familial. To obtain a copy of Alexander Dumas's *The Count of Monte Cristo*—of a higher literary order than the movies, pornography, or the comics— Brain must first obtain a half-crown. By depositing regularly a penny at a time with the bookseller, he at last attains his goal. It is then that even more formidable problems face him, for to break away from the cultural patterns of his parents is to insult and challenge their values, and it is this challenge that underlies the emotionally tense scene which occurs when Brian brings his book home. The heated exchange between parents and son has already been quoted in the biographical section of Chapter 1 and need not be repeated. The hard point of the incident is that Brian recognizes the justice of his partents' arguments: given their economic circumstances, he should not have purchased the book; it is an extravavance they cannot afford. But what Sillitoe stresses is that ignorance is a condition which Brian cannot afford, for it will lead to the same existence that his father has had, to Brian's children, and into future generations of Seatons. In addition to the economic difficulties, Brian must contend with a feeling that there is something "shameful" in reading, studying French, and drawing maps, for it means that he is separating himself from his family by a gulf that it cannot bridge. The fact is painful to him, but not to separate himself is to remain culturally and econmically imprisoned as his father is.

The beginning of the end of Brian's youth in Nottingham and of the idyllic existence which he has known at the Nook is signaled by the expansion of residential and commercial development to the boundaries of the Mertons' property. As Brian stands watching the ripping out of trees and bushes, the digging of drainage ditches, and the laying out of roads, his grandfather tells him that the building will probably not begin for a long time; but Brian soon witnesses the covering up of gardens, wheatfields, and football lots. In the fifteenth chapter, the last of the "Nimrod" section, he earns money by carrying tea to the laborers who are pouring the cement for the new construction.

Brian's last return to the Nook is marked by a painful awareness of change. The chimney of his grandfather's house is no longer visible from the point at which he has grown accustomed to seeing it. Only the foundations remain, covered by the rubble of broken glass and bricks, and interwoven by nettles which rise from the earth to catch his ankles. The garden has become a jungle without Merton's care, and the nearby homes are in a state of abandonment and decay: the doors are boarded, the windows smashed, and chimney pots tilting at an angle. The woods and the Cherry Orchard remain intact; but, as Brian is painfully aware, the voices of children are absent. Sillitoe approaches no nearer nostalgia than to say, "He stood still, unable to speak his thoughts that were too deep to be fished up by the bent pin of sentiment. But the disappearance of his friends disturbed him. . ." (198).

As Brian, too, pulls back from the past, he makes a wish "to go somewhere, a long way off, to jungles and mountains, and islands"—the sort of wish gods are fond of granting, but not with the result intended by the one who asks it. Sillitoe outlines his hero's future by noting that the Nook remained in the same state for a long time, "due to a war that had started. Its clear markings stayed until the war ended, and Brian didn't notice that it had been covered with prefabs until he came back from Malaya, by which time its obliteration was looked on as a good thing" (199).

IV *"Ropewalk"*

The third section, "Ropewalk," introduces several changes in the narrative. The novel jumps forward in time to pick up Brian's life at the age of nineteen in the military service, while the familiar setting of the Nook is displaced by the mountains and jungles of Malaya. There is also an abrupt change in tone. Sillitoe's depiction of Brian's youth, despite the struggles involved, bore the stamp of quiet recollection, with its portrayals of the rural life at the Nook, the rare but nonetheless genuine moments of harmony and affection among the Seatons, and Brian's discovery of the world about him, its people, and their way of life. During all this experience, Brian has been essentially passive, he is one who learns, who is more acted upon than acting. There has also been a quality of privacy in his child's world, such as we find in a passage from the last chapter of "Nimrod" in which Brian drinks from a stream running through the woods near the Nook: "Stones on the bottom were of different sizes and shades, with sand and green weed between, like a landscape, a miniature world under glass, uninhabited by minnows or waterboats: an ideal country of No-One-Else, ripe for filling and exploration" (198).

The transition from solitude to the communial military barracks, with their lack of privacy, and from innocence to the disillusioned

cynicism of an older Brian is an abrupt one. Sillitoe portrays him
writing a letter:

"Dear Mam,"—he looked at the envelope already addressed, ON
ACTIVE SERVICE scrawled across the top, which made him laugh
because the war had been over a good two years. I can't act, and I'm
nobody's bleeding servant . . . thanks for sending the Daily Mirrors. I
had a good read when I was on watch in my hut in the paddy field,
where I sit sending out morse code every day. I went to Pulau Timur
the other day and got drunk. I go once a month when I get paid. (204)

The tone of hostility and irony, Brian's bored dissatisfaction with his
work, and his drunkenness return us to the attitudes of *Saturday Night
and Sunday Morning,* but they lack both novelty and freshness in this
second rendering. Brian constructs in his imagination a data sheet of the
important aspects of his character; with few exceptions, the tone and
the details might apply equally to Arthur Seaton of the earlier novel:

Politics: Socialist; used to read *Soviet Weekly.*

Sex-life: Plenty until he fell foul of the authorities and received his two
years. Five fingered widow now.

Complexes: Mother, father, and inferiority.

Patriotism: Nil. Wants watching.

Favorite film star: Jeanne Crain.

Anything worthwhile: Good at wireless-operating and earns his six bob
a day. Works his sixty hours a week—so we
won't let him go yet.

Discipline: None. Even wears civvies on duty. (205)

Here is another young man of sexual prowess who is hostile toward
authority and bored with his work. The only significant change is that
Brian has adopted the label of Socialist, whereas Arthur remained
politically independent. In the last half of the novel, Sillitoe is
increasingly preoccupied with attacking England and with supporting
the Communist cause. Brian explains to his Malayan lover, Mimi, a
dance-hall girl, that his family had suffered deprivations during the
depression and that, as a consequence, he feels no loyalty to the English
government, which is to him a symbol of oppression. The more he
learns of Communist-supported opposition to British rule in Malaya,
the more he casts his loyalty with that opposition. As he understands

the situation, "the Malayan People's Anti-Japanese Army, supplied with arms during the war by the British, had now turned awkward and didn't want to give them back, were in fact becoming an anti-British army because they wanted independence" (230).

In order to supply a transition between the comparative innocence of Brian at the age of ten in "Nimrod" and the confirmed cynicism of Brian at the age of nineteen, Sillitoe in several chapters moves back in time to present Brian's first experiences as an industrial laborer in Nottingham at the age of fifteen, when he had obtained a job in Robinson's cardboard factory as an odd-job helper—running errands, sweeping out, lifting, and hauling. Once he had proved his worth, he was graduated to more difficult and more dangerous jobs. Sillitoe paints a grim picture of the conditions under which Brian works: rolls of paper are stacked "almost to the sprinkler valves," constituting a fire hazard; the manager of the factory allows Brian to work extra hours in violation of the Factory Act; and the work which Brian performs, cleaning soot from a stoke-hole-flue, is decidedly dangerous.

Sillitoe describes vividly the claustrophobic conditions of the task. In one instance, Brian pushes himself inside of a flue and finds it "black and suffocatingly warm. With one heave he was right in and flat on his stomach, taking care to drag the shovel and keep it by for when he needed to begin excavations . . . he went on for as far as he could go, his body and face almost immersed in the powder, nose eyes ears filled with it. He tried to turn round, and the discovery that he couldn't in the confined space sent a fear of panic through him" (237). He associates himself, in this underground existence, with the heroes from *The Count of Monte Cristo*: Jean Valjean fomenting revolution in the sewers of Paris; Edmond Dantes tunneling for freedom; and the physically confining working space—"the roof an inch or so above his head, and the wall on either side nudging at his elbows"—becomes symbolic of the social and economic confines of his class. The effect of the experience produces resentment in Brian, who recognizes that the pay which he receives is not commensurate with the hazardous nature of the work. For seventeen pence an hour now, he reflects, he is likely to condition his lungs for a case of tuberculosis later. His conviction is that employers as a group are unscrupulous in their use of their employees and that the British government, in failing to eliminate such circumstances, is unworthy of his loyalty.

Sillitoe moves Brian from this premise to a conception of Russia and communism as the best country and government for people of his own class. Elated, like all of England, over the German retreat from Moscow,

Brian reflects: "In full black flower, the Germans had gone goose-stepping into the land where all factories were owned by the people, and had made it grim and awful with starvation and suffering, a country which would one day become the promised land of the earth, where bread would be free and men would work only four hours a day" (239–40). The advance of the workingmen of Russia (for as such he regards the Soviet army) is for Brian a hope for an end to the exploitation of the working class by such factories as Robinson's. Sillitoe describes the practices of the company during the depression as having been deliberately unscrupulous: "Wage rates . . . set at a fraction above the dole, enough to give the incentive of a regular job, but hardly enough to keep its employees far from a harrowing experience of near starvation" (243). The relative prosperity brought on by the war has not, from Brian's point of view, changed the motivations of the company: "All they want is higher production and more money in their pockets. They can afford to be patriotic; so would I be. Rawson's supposed to be the best of 'em, but even he's a bastard" (249).

The theme of the chapter is escape, and Brian's last thought in his underground work place is "to get out of the earth, to see daylight and smell fresh air, to walk in the wind-thumped streets even if only to see the odd star above dark rooftops, to be out, away, a thousand miles off" (251). Like the miners in Emile Zola's *Germinal,* Brian has become through his laboring experience a "seed" of revolution.

V *"The Jungle"*

The title of the last section of the novel, "The Jungle" suggests the Malayan terrain and represents allegroically the circumstances of Brian and, presumably, of every man. The allegory develops during a journey which Brian and five other servicemen make to climb the "Mountain of the West"—Gunong Barat—which Sillitoe associates, as he clearly states, with the mountain that Dante attempts in vain to ascend in the first canto of the *Inferno.* In the novel, the journey is, on the realistic level, an exercise by a rescue group which Brian has helped form. From the beginning, however, the allegorical nature of the journey is suggested. Brian, who remains throughout the novel disdainful of belief in God, is awed by the beauty of Pulau Timur, the region which contains the mountain: "Who or whatever made this must have had good eyes, wielding his brush over such bays and washing broad streaks of sea around them; and a giant fist to punch the land so that hills came up from oblivion, the same hand throwing jewels along the valleys that turned into temples" (262).

Just before beginning the ascent up Gunong Barat, he recites to himself the opening lines of the *Inferno:*

> In the midway of this our mortal life,
> I found me in a gloomy wood astray,
> Gone from the path direct, And e'en to tell
> It were no easy task, how savage wild
> That forest, how robust and rough its growth . . .
>   scarce the ascent
> Began, when, lo! a panther, nimble, light,
> And covered with a speckled skin appeared . . .(329–30)

In Dante's work, climbing the mountain represents the soul's ascent to God through repentance. Dante learns that he cannot ascend the mountain directly through the Dark Wood (from a state of sin) when he is turned aside by a leopard, a lion, and a she-wolf—usually interpreted as representing the sins of lust, pride, and avarice. Guided by Virgil, the best of human reason, Dante must take the longer way through hell to see the capabilities of man's soul for evil. When he has traveled through the inferno, he can then repent of sin as he climbs Mount Purgatory and at last enter into heaven under the guidance of Beatrice.

Sillitoe's whole view of man is different. Brian has not sinned; therefore he has no need of repentance. Moreover, there is for him no God. Like Dante, Brian encounters a large feline, perhaps a tiger; but he manager to frighten it away with a shot from his rifle. If Brian is incontinent, Sillitoe suggests, it is because incontinence is a natural condition of man. If he is prideful, then that is a sign that he is of a spirited nature. Brian is not avaricious, for in Sillitoe's works, that is a sin peculiar to the rich. The jungle represents not moral darkness, but any unyielding object against which man pits his will and his strength. Accordingly, Brian's guide, Corporal Knotman, is not a man of surpassing reason; he is a man with great practical experience in dealing with the world of the jungle. While his rank is inferior to that of some in the group, all subordinate themselves to him; for the life of the jungle does not permit artificial distinctions.

Sillitoe's method is to introduce Dante's allegory only to reject Dante's philosophy. Brian, who begins the ascent imagining that his journey is to be a modern parallel to that of the great Florentine poet, soon comes to view the jungle and the mountain in quite a different light. Bereft of its allegorical significance, the jungle is to Brian a useless object unless it can be turned to some practical end: "he felt its spirit imposing too heavily on him, saw the jungle for the desert it was, a dull place because no one of flesh-and-blood lived there. All you could do was burn it down, let daylight and people in; otherwise it was only fabulous and interesting when written about in books for those who would never see it" (343). If it cannot provide a practical habitation for man, Brian concludes, then it is best left alone. The act of climbing the mountain at the last seems to him simply an "obsessive goal," something derived from the cinema and books, the legacy of an ancient cultural heritage which has lost its significance in the modern world.

Stopping in exhaustion before reaching the peak, all of the men agree that the mountain affords a pleasant view of the world below, but their desire and energy are not sufficient to take them on to the summit. Some dimly understood motivation urges Brian to complete the climb; he starts out alone to do so, but he is shortly turned back by a sluggish python which lies in the path. He feels fear at the sight of the serpent, turns away, and retreats "towards the others, no longer feeling alone in the jungle" (338). The point seems fairly clear: Sillitoe has employed Dante's symbols but has inverted their meaning. By attempting to ascend the peak, Brian has undertaken a useless task and has separated himself from humanity. That way lies evil, as the serpent suggests; for the only place for man is below, with his fellow man. Just before encountering the python, Brian had felt overcome by the "claustrophobic desolation" of the high place to which he had ascended; and he had turned his thoughts to the waterfalls and pools and to the noise of the stream far below; for those things now seemed to him a "sort of heaven" (338).

Like many of his contemporaries, Sillitoe's conception of heaven is earthly; his only theology, pragmatism. Turning his philosophy against the allegory which he has introduced, he finally has his hero question the value of the journey: "There's no point in climbing a mountain unless there's some purpose behind it, like to make a map or get food, collect wood or stake out a place to live . . . " (336). In short, Dante's allegorical ascent leads him to heaven; but Brian's leads him to the conviction that he should never have left civilization. In this respect, Sillitoe has shown himself to be a product of the modern age. As G. H. Bantock has observed in commenting upon the intellectual background of contemporary Western literature, "The Christian notion of man as inherently the child of sin, as belonging at once to the natural and to the transcendent world, and owing his possibilities of salvation to the Grace of God, a man whose essence is free self-determination and whose sin is the wrong use of his freedom, retains only an echo of its former vitality."[3]

The works of a writer like T. S. Eliot, to whom faith is vital, suggest that not Christianity but man has become impotent. In Sillitoe's works, the literary heritage of his Christian culture still makes itself felt, but its significance has been altered to accommodate the materialism of this age. Dante's conception of man as a rational being with free will, totally responsible for his choices for good or for evil, is in Sillitoe displaced by the concept of man as guiltless: he is, instead, a product of his environment and social class, a rational being whose choices and actions determine his fitness, not for heaven, but for the society of man.

Eschewing a facile resolution of the incident by returning the climbers to a pleasant reunion with their fellow men, Sillitoe stresses the fact that there is no easy escape from the earth and its problems. The sergeant who comes to pick them up at the base of Gunong Barat greets the men with the unsettling news that, while they have been gone, a war has been started by Malayan Communists, who are trying to force the British to leave the country.

Sillitoe uses the occasion of the Communist uprising in Malaya as a platform for political propaganda. The incidents and the attitudes presented in the last three chapters on Malaya are designed to present the Communist insurgents as the force of "right" and the British government as that of "wrong." To aid the Communists, Brian distorts radio signals so that the Communist transmitter cannot be destroyed; and, when he is supposed to be alert for distress signals from British aircraft, he turns down the volume on his radio and goes to sleep. The political message, of course, will inevitably be congenial to some readers and offensive to others.

The one spokesman for the opposition is Baker, who explains to Brian: "if anyone should rule Malaya it should be the Malays. They were already a long way to getting self-government anyway, though of course the Chinese would have a hand in it because they outnumbered other races in the peninsula and were the brains of the country. The Chinese Communists, Baker went on, reacting as expected to the emergency, were a small minority who wanted to get rid of the British and set up their own dictatorship. If you believe in democracy you've got to do what you can to put down these terrorists" (367-68).

The implication of the conclusion of the novel, however, rejects Baker's argument. When the climbing team returns to Gunong Barat in search of survivors from a downed aircraft, Brian confronts a Chinese Communist insurgent who charges him with a bayonet. Seaton subdues him; but, instead of killing the man, he sets him free, thinking: "I let him go because he was a comrade! I didn't kill him because he was a

man" (410-11). Later, when Seaton and his fellow soldiers are pinned
down by Communist fire, Brian refuses to fire back and shoots his
rounds into the air. The moral is apparently that communism is a
system of government so admirable that men should not hesitate to die
at the hands of those dedicated to it. The explanation cannot be that
Brian is simply opposed to violence; for, when the leader of the
expedition, Odgeson, threatens to report Seaton for insubordination,
Brian thinks: "I could put a bullet into his sanctimonious mug and
nobody would be the wiser. I can't think of any better reason for
carrying this lead-heavy rifle and fifty shells" (406).

The weakness in logic of the last section of *Key to the Door* arises
not so much from the political point being made as from Silitoe's
failing to provide a convincing psychological basis for Brian's convictions. To account for his not returning the fire of the insurgents, Seaton
must resort to such explanations as, "I'm making a present for Mimi.
. . . A goodbye gift in not shooting to kill maybe someone who, for all I
know, is the old boyfriend she had at high school in Singapore" (415).
We might reasonably have expected a writer of Sillitoe's talents to have
grasped at this stage of his career that propaganda usually makes poor
fiction—and that even good propaganda requires the persuasion of logic.

Although the last chapter of the novel is set in Malaya, Sillitoe gives
the reader a sense of returning to Nottingham by having Brian think of
people and places he has known there. He remembers what had been
told to him of his grandfather Merton's death, of the old blacksmith
walking to the place where the Cherry Orchard had been, of his getting
drenched in a thunder shower, and of his at last succumbing to
pneumonia. He thinks also nostalgically of his wife Pauline, of their
love, and of the pleasant prospect of returning to it. He even envisions
the domestic life which the future holds for him: "Pauline, go and buy
me a couple of pairs of overalls, an old jacket and a mashcan, a good
pair of boots to keep the suds and steel-shavings out. What number bus
do I need to get there spot on at half-past seven every morning? Don't
try and tell me; I was born knowing it" (436).

The return, however, is not merely to be a return to the past; but, as
the title suggests, the beginning of a new life to be effected, clearly,
through social reform. The conviction which he has reached at the end
of his tour of duty in Malaya is that "all men were brothers and that the
wealth of the world should be pooled and divided fairly among those
who worked, doctors and labourers, architects and mechanics" (432).
The Communists, he feels, have "an up-and-coming vision that our side

can never have any more. . . . a lot of the Communists are working-men like ourselves and know what's what" (426). This conviction is Brian's "key to the door"; the novel closes with Seaton's thought: "with the key to the door all you need do now, he smiled with an irony that made his heart constrict, was flex your labouring muscles and open it; though I wouldn't be surprised if that doesn't take more than half as long again" (439).

VI *Critical Evaluation*

The conclusion of the story suggests a new beginning rather than an ending; indeed; the last half of the novel marked a new direction in Silitoe's career, anticipating the tone and quality of his next two novels. The critical reaction to *Key to the Door* was tentative and conditional rather than simply negative. Most reviewers recognized that Sillitoe had, in the first two sections of the novel, captured reasonably well the awakening sensibilities of a youth born into the slums of Nottingham during the depression. The earlier chronicle of Arthur Seaton had captured the mood of a spirited and rebellious young man; but the story of Brian Seaton's childhood conveys the essence of working-class life. The first two sections are compelling, despite the fact that very little happens there that can be identified as "plot." There is little, too, in the way of philosophical questioning; yet Sillitoe makes the presentation of his people significant by the sheer force of his understanding of their thoughts and actions.

The critical reaction was tentative, however, for it is the whole novel that counts. Irving Howe, who praised the "rich evocation of life in an English industrial town during the depression years," noted the flaws as well: "As the story develops, however, Sillitoe fails to justify Seaton's concluding act. Nothing that has been shown to us, other than a few bare hints concerning Communist shop stewards in England, warrants the supposition that Seaton would refuse to shoot or would have any understanding as to why he refuses. More important, nothing in the novel indicates that Sillitoe himself has thought through the significance of the conclusion he provides. . . . Seaton does not refuse to shoot the guerrillas because they are fellow-beings; presumably, if they were of another political color, his hand would not tremble at the gun." [4] Howe's major objection is that Sillitoe has not taken the pains to think carefully about the changes which occur in Brian Seaton in the last half of the novel.

Walter Allen, who attempted to see *Key to the Door* as providing some clue to Sillitoe's growth as a novelist, concluded:

we are not likely to find a consistent development in Sillitoe, and this his new novel . . . confirms. As a novel, it it broken-backed; it falls into two roughly equal parts, each of which might be a separate work. . . . As a recreation of the industrial misery of the Thirties, the hopelessness, poverty, and squalor of urban life at the time, this part of the novel is brilliant. . . . Brian himself, however, seems to me insufficiently communicated. . . . *Key to the Door*, ambitious as it is, remains curiously tentative. It suggests that its author is still fumbling—though, remembering "Saturday Night and Sunday Morning" and "The Loneliness of the Long-distance Runner," it is difficult not to believe that before long he will be seen to have been fumbling to good purpose.[5]

Allen's prediction may well prove to be true, but it is doubtful that it has been proven to his satisfaction by Sillitoe's two subsequent novels, *The Death of William Posters* and *A Tree on Fire*.

CHAPTER 8

The Death of William Posters

I *The Dilemma of Frank Dawley*

Key to the Door ended with Brian Seaton, aged twenty-one, returning to his wife to begin the married life which his military obligation had postponed. *The Death of William Posters* opens with Frank Dawley, aged twenty-seven, leaving his wife to seek whatever adventures he may encounter. There is little, aside from the change of name, to suggest that Dawley is not simply an older Brian Seaton. At the age of twenty-one, Brian had already worked for four years in factories; Dawley, at twenty-seven, has put in twelve years at such labor. In addition, Dawley, like Brian, served in the military, made his home in Nottingham, and prided himself upon his interest in reading. The primary difference between them lies not in their attitudes but in their actions. Brian throughout his novel, remained largely passive even though he was dissatisfied with his circumstances. Dawley begins this novel seeking escape from his circumstances; indeed, escape into freedom is one of the major themes of the work.

The theme is embodied in an imaginary figure whom Dawley has conceived and named "Bill Posters," after the ubiquitous public signs, "Bill Posters Will Be Prosecuted." In Dawley's imagination, Posters is the archetype of the workman-underdog who, through persistence and endurance, rebels successfully against the social "system" and becomes, as the signs attest, the object of an intensive search. Posters is not simply of this age but of all preceding ages:

Who was General Ludd? None other than the shadowy William Posters, stockinger, leading on his gallant companies of Nottingham lads to smash all that machinery. In any case didn't Lord Byron make a stirring speech in the House of Lords about a certain William Posters sentenced to death in his absence for urging a crowd to resist yeomanry? Who set fire to Nottingham Castle during the Chartist riots? Later, who spat in

Lord Roberts' face when he led the victory parade in Nottingham after the Boer War? Who looted those shops in the General Strike? (18)

Thus, in Dawley's imagination, William Posters is the composite spirit of every rebel who has given the laboring classes hope; and the idea of such a figure leads Dawley to abandon his wife, children, home, job, and city—for those circumstances represent to him a trap which he finds himself no longer able to endure. No moral justification is given for Dawley's desertion, and neither Dawley nor the author seems to think one necessary. Both husband and wife are persuaded, in their brief encounter in the opening chapter, that there is no way for them to continue living together. Apparently, their love had degenerated into an unthinking, unfeeling routine revolving about eating, sleeping, working, and rearing their two children. Consequently, Frank bids his wife farewell and sets out upon the road.

After leaving home, Dawley, as he walks among the ruins of slums in the process of being demolished, thinks about the life he has determined to leave. Sillitoe artfully blends a description of the rubbled "ghetto of back-to-backs and narrow streets" with Frank's thoughts about his past. In his mind, a voice presents a composite of the advice he has received concerning the proper method of conducting his life: "No politics, lads, and no religion. Just drink your pints and sling your darts, heads down for Bingo and look alive to win a fiver in the end. When you're off sick we'll look after you, lad, give you a bit of club money, like, and a seaside booze-up once a year. But no religion, no politics. Don't think. Heads down. You're all free as long as you do as you're told. Legs eleven, bed and breakfast, key of the door. Heads down and look in, sink in that pound of treacle" (73).

Thus, Brian's Seaton's optimistic conviction that he had discovered the "key to the door" and need only to flex his laboring muscles to open it has become to Frank Dawley a hollow and meaningless hope. The labor, the home environment, the economic trap—all conspire to produce a quality of mind which is essentially sterile and conformist. It is from this sterile conformity that Dawley attempts to escape. Walking to the next street corner, he enters a pub, not yet fallen into disuse, where a few Saturday morning customers are gathered. They are of his own class, most of them elderly; and they seem to Dawley to be a preview of what he is to become, for they have traveled to the end of the laboring road which he has begun. They sit idly, speaking in low tones, playing at dominoes, looking now and again at "the comfortable vacancy of a half empty glass" (75), and drinking bad ale without complaint. When Frank tastes his, he asserts to the publican, "This ale's rotten. It's warm" (75).

Sillitoe turns this incident into allegory. The older customers, shocked and dumbfounded by the complaint, stop their activities, fall silent, and turn upon Frank "that concentrated stare kept by the old or finished for a member of the encroaching young, or a plain enemy with the expression of friend on his face" (76). They seem convinced that Dawley has challenged the value of their lives as well as the quality of the ale which they are willing to drink, and the affront becomes unbearable: Frank asks for a fresh glass of spirits, and when the publican adamantly refuses, Dawley slowly and deliberately pours the contents of his pint jar upon the floor. Shouts of "Set to him. . . He don't belong here," ring out, and the peaceful atmosphere of the pub is transformed into the hostility of a jungle. Frank strikes the publican and runs back toward the slum ruins pursued by the customers. He passes through the gutted remains of a house and into a back yard where he mounts the dilapidated roof of a lavatory building. The scene which ensues suggests a stoning ceremony in some primitive society:

A brick parapet divided the sloping roof of one set of lavatories from the slates of the next, and Frank stood precariously astride this high ridge—a ridge so rotten that he could bend down now and again to lift up a brick from it, or even a piece of one, to threaten his attackers—since they too had access to bricks and were now industriously prising them loose for a short-range stoning. . . .

A brick caught him weakly on the shoulder. He hurled two, clearing the space of backyards. The earth swayed again, his shoes moving slightly on the slates, several bricks cascading from the parapet between his legs. . . . He hurled the last brick through a window that still had glass, and at the force of his swinging arms the whole line of lavatories swayed like a slate-blue wave of the mid-ocean sea. His attackers drew back terrified into the house, as if running for their lives from some huge towering scar-faced monster high in the sky behind that Frank could not see. (78)

Sillitoe has conveyed in the scene a quality of animal brutality lurking beneath the veneer of civilized society. Dawley has been taught plainly by the incident that what most arouses the wrath of man is the suggestion of change. The pub customers may not like the ale they drink or the lives they lead, but they are transformed into bestial creatures when they are faced with a man who threatens to alter the status quo.

II *A Lesson in Love*

At the end of his first day of walking and hitchhiking across England, Dawley arrives at the home of a woman named Pat, a nurse in her early thirties who subsequently becomes his lover. Like Dawley, Pat has been married, has had an unsatisfactory experience at it, and, rather than sacrifice the remainder of her life to a bad cause, has left her husband and taken a position as a district nurse in a small community.

While Frank is living with Pat, he reflects upon the progress of his life. As with Sillitoe's earlier heroes, Arthur and Brian Seaton, life seems to Dawley something mechanistic, a series of conditioned responses leading toward a predetermined end. He notes that a young man goes through the experiences of school, work, and military service; then, after pursuing the ladies for awhile, he suddenly feels that he has confronted a wall and that it is within himself: "Then your eyes opened, or you thought they did, and in this wall you saw a hole at the bottom, surrounded by rubble and dust as if you'd used the hand grenade of your life so far to blast that hole just big enough to crawl through. So you got married" (36). Only later, after years of marriage, did the nature of his choice become clear to him. The wall had, in effect, "stayed a few feet at his back, and now, lately, it had drawn a circle around him, stifling his life, so that he had to get out or choke to death" (38).

The pattern is in essence the same that Sillitoe has used in his earlier works. In *Saturday Night and Sunday Morning,* the "wall" had been the monotony of Arthur's labor and his recognition of the impossibility of sustaining indefinitely the freedom of his bachelorhood. In *Key to the Door,* the "wall" had been for Brian his military obligation and the limitations which he conceived to be inherent in his social class. Arthur grudgingly accepted the repetitious work of a lathe operator and decided to end the aimlessness of his bachelorhood by marriage; Brian served out his military obligation and presumably returned to England to effect social reform.

In each case, the novel ends before the hero begins to live the new existence he has chosen for himself. We do not see Arthur Seaton married, nor do we see Brian effecting social reform; the future lies before them, and the reader is left with conviction that the heroes are still in the process of becoming. *The Death of William Posters* follows the same pattern, ending with Frank Dawley determined to become a member of the revolutionary Front de Libération Natonale in the Algerian revolt against French rule; but this novel has this important distinction: The hero rebels against his "wall" at the beginning of the novel, so that the bulk of the work is devoted to the hero's doing what he has not taken time to do during the first part of his life—finding out what sort of human being he is and what use he can be in the world. Frank Dawley is not a brawling drinker and seducer reveling out the last days of his premarital freedom, as was Arthur Seaton; and he is not a youth just approaching the threshold of maturity, as was Brian Seaton at the close of his novel. Frank is an adult, and his purposes are serious, as is the tone of most of the novel.

Dawley begins the process of self-discovery in his relationship with Pat, whose views are sufficiently different from his own to cause him to re-examine his beliefs, particularly regarding the "class" system in England and the nature of love between man and woman. Pat's sociological views are essentially "conservative"; she believes that people must bear individual responsibility for what they become. Her feeling is that work is the most important aspect of a person's life—"the only valid reason for being alive" (28); furthermore, to her "Everyone does the job they're fit for. The natural order of things works pretty well" (44). Those who work at jobs which they do not like are "too stupid, unintelligent, and cowardly to break the rut they're in and get work that they would like" (44).

Such a premise precludes any need for social reform, an assumption with which Dawley takes exception, since he, like other Sillitoe heroes, believes the social order of contemporary Britain is unjust. He objects that the present order is not "natural" and that those among the laboring classes who complain have ample reason to do so. He also feels that, if the workers had the "power of running things," they would reorganize the work so as to remove its "tredmill" quality and, as a consequence, no longer be driven to strike. This discussion does not lead to alteration in the beliefs of either Pat or Frank, but it does cause Dawley to think of social reform as an endeavor which could give his life meaning and direction.

His relationship with Pat also causes him to do some serious thinking about the nature of love. Despite Dawley's describing D. H. Lawrence's *Sons and Lovers* as a novel he had "read but finally didn't trust" and *Lady Chatterley's Lover* as a work which he had thrown on the fire in disgust, there are Lawrencian echoes in Sillitoe's description of the love which develops between Pat and Dawley: "He laid his hand on her wrist, squeezed it so that the veins met and hurt, held on as if the long hard grip were more necessary than the hour of unspoken words, a spiritual refuelling whose lifeline no words could latch into place. She felt something good in his touch, a desperate healing of interrupted blood-flow, a contact between them that no words were at the back of—and that maybe joined both their wounds" (67-68). Sillitoe does not, however, like Lawrence, insist that love is a mystical or quasi-religious experience. For Pat, love had to be grounded on a "strong, honest, mutual exchange of feelings" (69), while Dawley seems to feel that each lover must maintain a certain privacy of self apart from the other.

This and other differences finally lead to an end to their relationship. Dawley maintains that "A family kills you; it kills everybody, I think, the way it drags down your spirit unnecessarily"; but for Pat, rearing a family is "the only way to live" (97). The disagreement finally devolves into a heated argument, in which Pat asserts that a person who is truly in love thinks of his lover first and of himself second, an attitude which Dawley rejects, terming it "self-sacrifice." It is not really self-sacrifice which bothers him, however, so much as the idea of sacrificing self for just one other person. He senses a larger obligation: "People should adjust themselves to the external world, not to each other, a diffuse connection with the whole world rather than with the icy inbite of destruction. There is a natural tenderness in everybody which should make it possible for man and wife—or woman and man—to take care of each other, and ignore the fastenings of overstrung emotion which strangle at both of them" (105). This conclusion paves the way for Dawley's decision at the end of the novel to dedicate himself to revolution and social reform.

III   *The Workingman as Revolutionary*

After describing Dawley's farewell to Pat, Sillitoe introduces a long disgressive episode in which Dawley becomes a close friend of an eccentric painter, Albert Handley, who shares Dawley's views on the oppression of the workingman. Through Handley, Dawley meets his next lover, Myra Bassingfield, who decides to escape her unhappy marriage by accompanying Dawley on a trip to Spain. While Frank does not specify any particular reason for making the journey, it is clear that he wants to become involved in political revolution, and Sillitoe soon provides him with an opportunity to do so.

On the ship bound from Barcelona to Majorca, Dawley encounters a young American named Shelley Jones who has been engaged in revolutionary activities in Cuba and is looking for similar employment in Europe. When Shelley asks what Dawley is looking for, he replies, "A world to build, maybe" (253), adding that he would not be averse to tearing down a few governments before starting to build. Dawley expresses his dissatisfaction with the rationality of modern man by saying, "As soon as we get enough bread and cheese in us we have to start looking for a soul. It's a waste of time though" (252). Later, he elaborates on the point in a conversation with an American writer named Larry. In response to the writer's calling Dawley an "Uncomplicated Person," Frank gives a rather succinct explanation of his materialistic philosophy:

I'm the empty man, the man without religion. All I believe in is houses and factories, food and power-stations, bridges and coalmines and death, turning millions of things out on a machine that people can use, people who also turn out millions of things that other people can use. It's no use harping back to poaching rights and cottage industries. We've got to forget all that and come to terms with cities and machines and moon landings. We're going to become new men, whether we like it or not, and I know I'm going to like it. (259)

When asked if the "new men" will have to lose their souls in the process of coming to terms with cities, machines, and moon landings, Dawley replies:

What soul? Still, if you want to put it like that, you can. All the space that's left by kicking out the soul is taken by a railway, a hammer, a whole landscape of industrial and material necessity. The soul is so big that you can get all those things in, and more. The bum-bailiffs march up to the soul and sling God out kicking and screaming. Then the real things of life move in, and the space that God inhabited (all his bloody mansions) is enormous. We can get so much in there. (260)

The position is fervently stated; but, even as a solution to the problems presented in this novel, it is not convincing. The environment of "houses and factories, food and power-stations," the "turning millions of things out on a machine that people can use," is the very milieu from which Dawley has just escaped, and which all of Sillitoe's heroes have disliked. The houses become filled with "kidnoise"; the factories with monotonous labor and an unsatisfactory managerial staff; the mass-produced food is unsavory; and the power stations, in addition to doing other things, send out the innocuous television programs to which Sillitoe is so averse. The author seems to have placed his hero in the position of both advocating and rebelling against the same thing.

The second part of Dawley's reply, that the aspect of man formerly concerned with God and the soul should be displaced by "material necessity," seems to evade the central question of the novel—Dawley's search for identity and purpose—by assuming that the basic cause of man's difficulties arises from his contradictory inclinations toward religion and materialism. In terms of Dawley's own circumstances, such a conflict seems to be a misstatement of the problem, for he is from the beginning a man without religion.

The contradictions in philosophy are resolved to some extent by Dawley's further reflections upon them. As Frank and Myra live together in Majorca, then in Granada, he begins to note an alteration in their relationship, as well as an end to his old conceptions of love, which, he concludes, had been based primarily upon mutual destruction. Forming between them is a new relationship which would "enable a man and woman to live in equality, with regard and respect for each other's purpose in the world" (268). He comes to recognize that a man and woman "must love more people than just each other. The old idea of love is sliding away from the fingertips of the new man, like a thousand-colored ferry boat heading for the open sea" (272). Thus, Dawley has already modified his initial philosophy of simple materialism. The production of "factories, food, and power-stations" will still figure importantly in his struggle, but they will no longer be ends in themselves. Rather, they will be the end product of his larger obligation to his fellow man.

Rejecting Jean Paul Sartre's thesis in *No Exit,* Dawley asserts, "Hell wasn't other people; it was the inability to work, to act, to do" (272). Having recognized some purpose in life, he overcomes one difficulty which perplexed him at the beginning of the novel—his concern over the possibility of mass nuclear destruction: "Death was nothing to write home about, to dwell on, think of. The shell went through you, the hydrogen bomb flashed you up, old age put you to sleep" (272), but the fear of death is of consequence as long as a man is doing something with his life. In sum, "The new man of the world must work and live as if he weren't going to be alive the next day" (272).

How Dawley puts his new philosophy to work is perhaps the greatest weakness of the novel. In Tangier, where he has taken Myra to have her child by him, Dawley again encounters the American revolutionary Shelley Jones, who has become involved in the Algerian rebellion against France. When Jones explains to Frank that the forces of the Front de

Libération Nationale are losing and need arms, supplies, and men, Frank agrees, "after a bare minute of packed thought," to assist in smuggling arms to them. It is never made clear precisely that Dawley knows of the merits of fighting for one side or the other. Presumably, he is acting on the principle which he had expressed to Shelley a few pages earlier, that happiness is "doing work for yourself that at the same time is helping other people" (286). Moreover, he feels that there is a "natural connection" between the work which he had done in the factories and the work which he will be doing in Algeria, since both help the "proletariat." There is no questioning Dawley's sincerity, but his judgment seems to be based on impulse.

Frank and Shelley make a dangerous and suspenseful journey with their cargo of arms through the desert wastes. When they must at last stop for fear that the daylight will reveal them to French planes, they set up an ambush against the possibility that they will be discovered by ground troops. With his gun at his shoulder, Frank reflects, "I'm waiting in case the French show up, when I'd give a lot for it to be the British, because they are the ones I should be doing my nut against" (308). The patrol which finally wanders into their ambush is neither French nor British but German, hired as mercenaries by the French. As Dawley waits, he reflects upon the image of William Posters which has been with him since his youth: "that soul-anchor stuck in your craw, those dim jerking pictures flickering on the screen behind your eyes when closed, working bewildering renegade rebel magic on the sentimental layers of your caked heart . . ." (309); Frank envisions Poster's death, even imagines himself as leading Posters to his destruction, because the new life which he has undertaken does not leave room for the old images which gave him courage when he based his life on the assumption "that whatever he wanted was unattainable" (310).

Bill Posters was, in fact, an image suited to a philosophy of despair, a vision "flitting from wall to shadow whither your own demons pursued you in an ever narrowing maze with misery and failure at the middle" (311). In Frank's imagination, Posters dies "the multiple dream-deaths that a hero deserves," but, when Frank has himself been the agent of death for one or more of the patrol of German mercenaries, Posters is heard of no more, for he belongs with Dawley's past. Dawley's commitment from that point forward is to the revolution and to the future: "Something in him was going to be reconstructed," the author promises; precisely *what* is left to the sequel to the novel, *A Tree on Fire*.

IV   *Critical Evaluation*

The reception of *The Death of William Posters* was not enthusiastic, nor should it have been. Reviewers pointed out difficulties in Sillitoe's style, in the conception of his hero, and in the implications of the work. For Frank Kermode, the basic weakness of the novel lay in its commitment to violence:

Sillitoe's style is one of habitual violence, a deliberate reflection of the hated, cheated prole, crossed by a certain awkward artifice, which is correlative with the hero's self-education. It is clear that the maintenance of this stylistic attitude presents him with enormous problems. There is evidence of slackness, fatigue; there is the practical difficulty of making fights violent when everything else is violent. . . .It seems characteristic that the best writing in Sillitoe's last two novels comes at a time of the heroes' self-expression in action, and in a context of guerrilla warfare.

Paul Levine objected to Sillitoe's conception of and attitude toward Frank Dawley:

Behind all the detail is Sillitoe's frank admiration for his hero, the feeling that Lawrence had for Mellors and Hemingway had for Robert Jordan. Like Lawrence, Sillitoe is concerned with the modern feelings of alienation from meaningful work and sex; like Hemingway, he is bothered by the limitations of heroism in an overcivilized society. And like both at their worst, Sillitoe goes about showing his concern with a solemn and numbing earnestness which makes him take his hero more seriously than we can.[2]

John W. Aldridge saw the weakness of *The Death of William Posters* as a reflection of larger problems which Sillitoe faces in his development as a writer: "Sillitoe's trouble has always been that he knows—or once knew—only one thing really well: what it is like to grow up in the English industrial slums. This experience provided him with a set of limited attitudes toward society—which, when first formed, were solidly grounded in the facts of life as he saw them. But, as is so often the case with writers of this type, the passage of time did not provide him with any comparably significant new experience. It simply dimmed his relation to the old."[3]

Aldridge's observations are persuasive, although speculative. There is no reason to assume that Sillitoe has had no "significant new experience" since writing his early works, but it is clear that he has been unable to transform his experiences, or his imaginative thought, into successful fiction in this novel. There are too many inconsistencies in Dawley's conception of his problem and in his resolution of it, and—with the exception of a few scenes in the novel—the author has paid too little attention to creating a sense of reality in the work.

CHAPTER 9

A Tree on Fire

I   *Middle-aged Eccentricity*

A Tree on Fire, written in London and Majorca between 1964 and 1965, is the sequel to *The Death of William Posters.* In the sequel, Sillitoe develops the exploits of Frank Dawley in the French-Algerian war and carries still further his philosophy of revolution. The novel opens with Myra returning to England with Mark (the four-week-old son whom Dawley has fathered) after having waited more than two months for Frank to return from the desert fighting. Upon arriving in England, she is met by a character from the earlier novel, Albert Handley, who in this work is one of the major spokesmen for Sillitoe's anti-British sentiment. Handley rails against the customs officials, asserts that he would like to be deported, and in general conducts himself like an eccentric middle-aged rebel. His eccentricity seems to be almost conventional in nature, however.

The "primitive" painter Handley of the earlier novel has become famous and wealthy, but he remains as irascible as ever, mocking the art critics, dealers, and painters who now pursue and flatter him. His house is called "The Gallery," and, the narrator tells us, "often he didn't know whether one might call it an art gallery, a rogues' gallery, or a shooting gallery, though mostly it was a bit of all three rolled into one madhouse" (26).

Handley's children are involved in various mad pursuits: one son, Richard, has one of the walls of his room covered with military maps of England and Wales, with special details of atomic establishments and bomber bases, and on another wall a huge Algerian Front de Libération Nationale banner hangs. In this room Handley and his son create a fantasy world of revolution in which they imagine that insurgents are battling against British troops. In Sillitoe's early work—particularly in the stories of *The Loneliness of the Long-distance Runner*—he drew a sharp distinction between illusion and reality, stressing the necessity of a man's avoiding the world of illusion. In portions of this work, he seems to have moved closer to that fantasy world himself, allowing the Handleys to create in their imagination the British civil war which Sillitoe has put forward throughout his work as an extreme solution for the social ills which plague his country. The difference is that in the early fiction, Sillitoe focused upon the lives of laboring people; he set their world in opposition to the managers, owners, and government officials with whom they had to deal to survive. In that context, the desire for revolution on the part of the laboring class seemed a natural reaction to the difficulties of their existence.

But in *A Tree on Fire,* Sillitoe has moved away from his former presentation of the lives of the lower economic classes. Handley is wealthy, and there is no indication that he suffers from oppression of any sort. His hostility really seems to be directed against all who lead "normal" lives; he asserts: "Grown-up, mature people are ten-a-penny. They're all over the place, like flies in summer, strong-faced vacuous venomous pipe-smokers and happy savers and careful drivers. Don't talk to me about the lumpen living-dead. Put them in a room with a strong light and they'd start to confess" (74).

Handley's aggressive hostility is indicative of the fact that Sillitoe seems to be more and more inclined to express himself only through metaphors of violence, revolution, and death. Chapter 10 presents Handley contemplating the subject of his next painting. While his studio is located in the peaceful rural surroundings of Lincolnshire, his thoughts are dominated by scenes of battle:

The biggest colour began as green, fields, oases, valleys, seaweed and estuary, life-perpetuation, love in the environs of Venice and Voronezh, vile green effluvia falling from bomb canisters lobbed on paddy-fields, lodged in ditches where green men were fighting or burning (a change of colour here towards yellow, orange, saffron robes of Buddhist monks firing modern and complex artillery with deadly precision from fortified pagodas) or flashpanning out over hamlets from which men have fled but women and children cannot. Green gas yellowing over green fields to destroy all seeds and shoots of life. A leg goes green, gangrene, dead green and livid, jealousy of green by those who are dead for the living flowers of people unconscious in life but full of work and struggle in that humid green forest, blistering enmouldering green, emerald of defeat for the iron merchants and industrial strong whose chewing-gum tastes of spite and who try to belt down the guerrilla men and women of the coming world. (100-101)

II   *A Visionary in the Desert*

In Part Two, Sillitoe shifts the scene to the Algerian war and
Dawley's involvement in the revolutionary struggle against the French.
The dominant images suggest the aridity of the desert soil, but they also
stress the tenacity of all things which live upon it. Sillitoe sees in the
desert a life force which can withstand the onslaught of any hostile
force, including the superior French military forces. In the opening
scene of Part Two, Dawley witnesses the event which gives the novel its
title. At some unspecified location in the desert at night, Frank hears
the drone of an airplane and flattens himself against the soil. He then
observes a tree which is inflamed by a bomb dropped from the plane:
"A tree was burning on a hillside, a single tree in a waste of sand and
ash. They knew it well, had used it as a landmark when counter-moving
for the last three days to outwit a French motorized patrol from the
west. The tree had been dead for a long time but clung to the red
friable substance half way between dry sand and bitter soil, scrubbed
and bitten clean by passing camels, picked at by nomads for teafires
after dusk. No one could say when it had last borne leaves" (145).

The tree has both strategic and symbolic importance to the
revolutionaries: due to its solitary and elevated position, it is a valuable
geographic reference point; and the fact that it still proves useful and
refuses to succumb long after it is dead serves to remind the
revolutionaries of the spirit which they must have in order to attain
victory against the forces of the French. Frank, intrigued by the
burning tree, watches until the main branches and the trunk fall; then
his thoughts carry him to a significance beyond the simple destruction
of natural life by instruments of war. He remembers that he has
observed the remains of other trees destroyed by bombs, and he recalls
that they are never utterly removed from the earth, for the stumps
remain: "He'd seen trees similarly blasted in a grove near Aflou. . . .
Yet, an anaemic green shoot always grew from part of the sheltered
base. It was hard to understand why they were so bent on survival,
though looking at them, it seemed that it was not in their power to ask
such a question" (148). As Frank discovers, a similar will to survive
pervades the Algerian revolutionaries and, even when they are bombed
out and seem to be destroyed, there arises another "anaemic green
shoot" to continue the cycle of existence.

The struggle of the Algerians is only part of the subject of Sillitoe's
novel, however. An equally important topic is Frank Dawley's

continuing search for self-identity and purpose. In his early works, Sillitoe's characters find themselves in economic circumstances which require that they use cunning to make their way in the world, but Dawley is given greater freedom of choice. He rejects a secure, comfortable, and uneventful existence and abandons Myra in order to act positively within the world to accomplish something for others. In "The Loneliness of the Long-distance Runner" and in *Saturday Night and Sunday Morning,* there is a greater sense of entrapment: a man can struggle but he cannot win. Smith refuses to yield to the system of the "In-laws," and he murmurs threats against them; but there is no sense of his positively escaping the system or of his creating terms of existence acceptable to himself. His essence is always circumscribed by the system which he cannot accept or escape. The same is true of Arthur Seaton, who gains his freedom on Saturdays and Sundays but finds the other five days a dreary monotony. The reader may have a sense of Arthur's having attained some degree of maturity in his final decision to marry; but, from Arthur's point of view, the decision is a type of succumbing: "Whenever you caught a fish, the fish caught you" (236).

Frank Dawley is less subject to an unalterable fate. He escapes the traps of factory and a deadening marriage; and, in the desert, he is conscious of having attained a victory over fate. The problem with his newly won freedom is that he soon abandons it in order to dedicate himself to the cause of world revolution. He thinks, "I am for progress, progress at any price, but when the world is socialist—then what? Yet I can't say: 'Then what?' until all the world *is* socialist or socialized. And since it will probably take more than my life and lifetime, what's the point of asking 'Then what?' Perhaps there is a point, and that when socialism is achieved (if that's the word), we'll be free in our spare time to indulge in private mysticism: Zen masters, Zen commissars, Zen Stakhanovites. Even collective mysticism" (227).

Conceiving of some goal beyond material plenty for everyone is obviously a task which leads Dawley into difficulty. It may be, however, that Sillitoe is suggesting, like Dostoevsky's Grand Inquisitor, that freedom is an illusion which man finds attractive in his imagination but unbearable in attainment. Dawley's sense of freedom exists only while he is in the process of breaking away from his former life. When he has committed himself to the cause of revolution, he again thinks of freedom as residing somewhere in the future, after the goal of world socialism has been accomplished.

III   *The Polemics of Madness*

Part Three returns to England and to the story of the Handley family and Myra, but the various episodes of Handley, his wife, and his children need not be detailed since they have so little relevance to the main argument of the novel. The strongest connecting link between this section and Dawley's story is the brother of Albert Handley. During World War II, John Handley had been captured by the Japanese and held in a Singapore prison camp where he had formed with other British prisoners a "left-wing group . . . to produce a sort of newspaper, in opposition to the British officers as well as the Japanese" and to give "secret lectures on militarism and the class-war" (42). During the fifteen years following the close of the war, he confined himself to his brother's house where he spent his time transcribing radio messages of various revolutionary groups and filling his notebooks with vituperative polemics. Sillitoe presents a generous sampling:

The American rocket and bomber bases must be treated as were German bases in occupied France during the war. Adopt the attitudes of the French Resistance to the Nazis. And not only the land of the bases, but also the land of the fox-hunters must come under the hammer. The police, the armed forces, civil defence personnel are an army of occupation. Those who join their ranks are traitors. Those who hold state secrets and do not try to divulge them to an enemy or to make them public knowledge are also traitors. (291)

At another point, property ownership comes under attack:

Everything on your back, feet, in your mouth was common property. There was to be no ownership whatsoever, and no state to distribute it either. Your house was everyone's house, provided everyone's house was your house. Abolish private property, and you abolish privacy, for who would want privacy if they had no property. Privacy is privacy. The prime sin of the world was the ability and opportunity to possess, to have and to hold until the heart grew cold and became an object from which all evil sprang. (293)

The confused ramblings of John Handley suggest rather clearly that he is deranged, but there is no indication that Sillitoe wishes for the reader to dismiss Handley's proposals and opinions as the ravings of a madman. To the contrary, Handley is revered by the principal characters in the novel; and he has the important function of providing advertisements for Frank Dawley, whom he describes as one of those men "helping in some unrewarded, idealistic, mystical way to bring about the unification of the world. In the future they may become the new yet unacknowledged saints, men who went into the desert, fasted by necessity, fought by conviction, and died by faith. . . . For a truly religious man the light can never fail, and if universalism becomes a religion and socialism is the way we have chosen to bring it about then even the mistakes and the tragedies of socialism have to become acceptable" (330).

John Handley's equating revolutionary activities with sainthood, mysticism, and faith may seem, out of context, to be an extreme position; but, in fact, it is a thesis presented more than once in the novel. Dawley's closest companion in the Algerian war, the American Shelley Jones, is a zealous, chauvinistic apostle of revolution who summarizes his philosophy as follows:

Evil is no mystifying concept. It is the inability to change for the good. It is being slothful among bad conditions of life, and preaching that the acceptance of present suffering makes the adventure of change unnecessary, thereby implying that suffering is sufficient adventure for the soul. One must prove that it is not—by making it possible for the weak to inherit the earth and become strong, and to use their newly-won strength in order to help those still weak in the world, which is no less than the fight for eternal justice, a uniting of mankind to give everyone equality and food and dignity that will enable them to become individuals in a universal sense. The tree must purify and burn, shed its leaves in the fires of insurrection. (195)

In the philosophy of Shelley Jones, as in that of John Handley, there is a uniting of religious and political fanaticism. The narrator attempts to remain aloof from their views, but the reader inevitably builds a conception of the "implied author"—to use Wayne Booth's term—of this and every novel. If John Handley can be dismissed as a madman and Shelley Jones as an impetuous, hot-headed youth, it is impossible to read Albert Handley as being anything other than a character who has the sympathy of the author; for Albert, too, conceives of revolution as a religious quest: "Frank's no idealist . . . but a workman who saw the futility of his life and used his energy to try and lift others out of their suffering. He's on the right side, in spite of his using the revolution as a spiritual quest, like most of us. Revolution is the only remaining road of spiritual advance" (308-19). The narrator refrains from overtly praising his hero, but he achieves that end through such comments as Handley's. He also creates an inescapable political "message" within the novel by having the foregoing characters repeatedly espouse their philosophy of revolution.

IV   *A Paean to Violence*

Sillitoe connects the England and Algeria episodes by having John Handley set out on a journey to locate Frank Dawley. In Part Four, as the setting shifts once more to Algeria, Dawley is portrayed while recuperating from a feverish illness which keeps him confined to a bed in a small village for ten days. The convalescence provides him with an opportunity to evaluate his past actions and philosophy, and he concludes that some revision is in order:

When the foul and useless love you had been conditioned to accept by a finished and rotten society dead in its tracks had died, and you knew that to love only one person out of all others in the world, and be yourself loved by someone else out of all others in the world was wrong in every sense, then you began to experience a new warmth of life, a responsible manifold feeling towards all others and not just one. The love of one was the love of death and of the devil. The love of all was a respect for creation. You could not love only one person in the desert, because if you did you and everyone would perish. There was a love in which the phallus dominated all else, the boss and operating member tyrannising over everything you did or wanted to do. The other love was controlled by the hands that helped, taught, built and if necessary fought. The phallus could not be ignored, but neither could it be allowed to dominate, for such a domination was destruction leading you to the sinkpots and gutters of the earth, dropping you and everyone through to the cloacae of oblivion. (358-59)

Dawley's rejection of sensuality contrasts sharply with the concupiscence which characterized Arthur Seaton, the hero of Sillitoe's first novel, written almost a decade before *A Tree on Fire.* Just as remarkable is the shift from Seaton's spirited independent egoism to Dawley's self-effacing and beneficent dedication to the common good. The problem with Dawley's quasi-Christian philosophy, of course, is that he personally does not approach anything resembling a "manifold feeling toward all others." He loves his fellow revolutionaries and the economically deprived, but he hates passionately "the haves." Sillitoe has altered the dedication of his hero, but he has kept intact the old animosities.

When John Handley locates Dawley in a field hospital, he urges him to return to England for Myra's sake. Dawley, who has already been considering returning in order to gain financial support for the revolution, agrees to do so. In Part Five, the two board a ship and travel to Paris, where they part company; Handley, afraid of air travel, stays behind to await passage on a ship while Dawley flies on to England. Sillitoe uses the occasion to launch one final attack upon his country by presenting John's thoughts aboard ship. Blaming England for having sent him in his youth to fight in Malaya, John reflects, "the English were an island people who had once been thrown into temporary greatness by a hundred-year bout of energy. They were insular plain-speakers once more who muddled through by clan and hierarchy, the eternal mean categorisation of a rattled elite, and a dead bourgeoisie, and the people who knew their place because they had taken into their systems the poison of centuries from this so-called elite, and into their bodies the serf-bones of degredation" (415). As the cliffs of England come into view, Handley commits suicide.

This melodramatic event is used to underscore the guilt which Sillitoe feels England should bear for sending its young men to war. It is also the occasion for Dawley's general indictment of the English class system. Resenting the official explanation of Handley's death in the inquest report—"suicide while of unsound mind"—Dawley thinks, "No other verdict was possible. The lumpen-bourgeoisie demanded it. It had to be suicide if they were to keep their confidence and survive. The idea of actually choosing death in opposition to the best of all possible lives that they offered was alien to them. Well, they could keep it until it was ripped away from them by machine-guns and Molotov cocktails. The one infallible answer was always violence, violence, and still more violence. In Algeria it was already succeeding in what it set out to do. It couldn't fail, provided it was prolonged and violent enough" (432). Soon after Dawley expresses this thought, the novel is brought to a close, with Dawley, his wife Nancy, his lover Myra, his children by both women, and the Handley family joining together to establish, as Albert expresses it, a "community as a memorial to my brother John, and to his life, such as you all know it was" (446).

V   *Critical Evaluation*

A Tree on Fire is not without literary merit. In the Algerian sections Sillitoe portrays convincingly the environment of war, the pain of being wounded, the senseless suffering of the civilian population, and the cunning and daring upon which the lives of guerrilla fighters must depend. Sillitoe's realism is much the same type that we find in a novel,

like Ernest Hemingway's *For Whom the Bell Tolls.* Sillitoe's novel, however, is seriously marred by the leftist propaganda and by the paean to
violence which it conveys.

Critical reaction to the novel has been cool. Robert Taubman's
observations are representative:

The northern, sociological Sillitoe, if he ever existed, has disappeared.
He deserves the reputation for anger which he acquired in the Fifties:
only it now looks like anger of an older kind, that goes with an England
divided against herself, factory acts, class-struggle and sex-struggle. . . .
Spiritual energy—or simply energy—is the vision which Sillitoe offers.
It's what England lacks; and the novel is obsessed with England, "the
maggoty home-land," though not often directly. . . . He insists too
much on art and revolt, eternal conflict, energy—the vision he seems to
share with his characters. The real interest surely lies not with visions or
acts of desperation but with what provokes them—the emptiness that
demands to be filled somehow: with art or energy, with other worlds if
necessary, or just noise.[1]

The difference in the quality of Sillitoe's earlier and later fictional
efforts is perhaps accounted for in a comment which Albert Handley
makes in the early pages of *A Tree on Fire.* For the artist, he observes,
"Success is a funny thing: can eat your guts out. But the secret of
beating such an enemy is not to regard it as success, to keep on thinking
of yourself as an exiled, unemployed nobody" (16). Sillitoe seems to
have taken the advice to heart—it may be good advice for some—but his
personal sense of exile seems to be grounded in a bitterness and in a
hatred of his country that has diminished his art rather than elevated it,
as it did James Joyce's. In Sillitoe's earlier works, there is an
exceptional rendering of a tragic and Classical sense of fate: his
characters sense that they may not be destined to "win," now, in
economic or legal terms; yet they battle on with a spirited, fustian
vainglory that is in itself a victory of the human spirit.

In his most recent novels, Sillitoe has abandoned this sense of fate
and adopted a determination to win through armed rebellion the
economic and social battles in which his heroes are engaged. From the
heroes' point of view, and from the author's, this rebellion is good,
politically, economically, and philosophically; from the critic's point of
view, aesthetically, it is not, for the winning of these battles seems to be
expressible only in terms of martial "liberation." In *A Tree on Fire* this
conviction so occupies the center of the stage that the characters seem
to become minor attendants serving the Lord of Revolution. When that

happens, the fine tragic mood which the author is capable of creating and the engaging spirit of his heroes devolve into social thesis. What was art becomes simply propaganda. We hope that in his future works Sillitoe will regain the quality of his early writings, particularly of his short stories, and that his preoccupation with political commitment will give way to a preoccupation with art.

CHAPTER 10

Revolutionary and Poet

T HIS study has thus far been limited to a consideration of Sillitoe's
accomplishments as a writer of fiction, for it is primarily in this
capacity that he has gained prominence in contemporary British
literature. He has published three volumes of poetry, however: *The
Rats and Other Poems, A Falling Out of Love and Other Poems,* and
Love in the Environs of Voronezh. Various poems in the collections
should be considered, some because of the light which they throw upon
his fiction, others because they are good in their own right.
Furthermore, the writing of poetry is for Sillitoe far from being an
ancillary activity to the writing of prose. In commenting on his literary
career, he has observed, "I consider myself a poet more than a writer of
prose...."[1] While the reading public does not now concur, it may alter
its opinion if the quality of Sillitoe's verse continues in the direction it
has taken in his most recent publication, *Love in the Environs of
Voronezh.*

I   *The Rats and Other Poems*

Sillitoe wrote the title poem of his first collection of verse between
1956 and 1957, at the same time that he was composing *Saturday
Night and Sunday Morning* and such stories as "On Saturday
Afternoon" and "Noah's Ark." "The Rats" expresses unequivocally in
poetry the political convictions that Sillitoe did not choose to convey
with such candor in his fiction until ten years later with the publication
of *A Tree on Fire.*

Sillitoe begins his long poem (fifty-seven pages in the W. H. Allen
edition) by expressing astonishment at the alteration of international
political alignments since the end of World War II. In 1945, he
observes, the English regarded the Russians as their friends, the
Germans as their enemies. The poet finds it impossible to change his
own attitudes so drastically. He remembers "those Russians who bled

in raw / Winds to save us" and casts a suspicious eye upon "fine brave Nazis wanting another go" (17). The Englishmen who "remember fighting large / And blindly for 'democracy' " (16) now feel that the society to which they have returned is not democracy; but they have no spirit for revolution. The narrator's attitude toward his fellow Englishmen is frankly paternalistic: he sees them as a race made so dull by television and by the daily routine of working that they are incapable of using their own initiative to "test the loaded yoke / By a gaze to heaven, when all earthly bread / Is planted firmly at their feet instead" (19). His purpose, as he conceives it, is to arouse their sensibilities and stir them to revolution, which is the major argument of the poem.

Sillitoe begins by defining the terms which he intends to use to represent the principals of the conflict, "rats" and "Ogads ":

> The rats are government, and Ogads slaves
> Who know not where they go nor what road paves
> The way to Revolution. Such holy ritual
> Is lost on Ogads resting in habitual
> Stupor—is an ancient elixir of home
> For on-the-run Philosophers. (20)

Sillitoe seems to equate revolution with life itself. To conform, to accept the norms of society, is for him the equivalent of spiritual death:

> Revolution is the word of God
> A firefly that lifts from soddened ground
> For one second at the end of spring.
> ....
> These are the commandments of the rats:
> You shall be born into the melting-vats
> Without an eye to give or a tooth to lose
> And never want for schooling, work or shoes.
> Good; but each advertisement is a decree
> A hanged man on the propaganda tree
> to make it shoot up high and thin:
> A hundred thousand may begin
> To march one damp October dawn:
> Find a Lenin waiting at Victoria Station
> Uttering incandescent incantation. (22)

Sillitoe's revolutionary creed seems to arise from a sense of boredom, or perhaps from a fear of lethargy, rather than from some clearly defined intention to right social conditions which he feels are insufferable. It is just the idea of accepting a peaceful existence—even with material comfort—which arouses his wrath:

> You shall love the rats who take the hours
> From your clumsy hands, who guide you over roads
> And traffic islands, take the heavy loads
> From lighter brains, and give you paper flowers ˙
> Of happiness, and stand you in a line
> For bus or train, transport you to a house
> And television-set and Ogad wine:
> You too can be a rat divine
> A living civil-servant of a louse,
> Though first you must become a mouse. (22-23)

Inevitably, the appeal of such a revolutionary "hymn" loses much of its force in the absence of some clear indication of oppression. The "Radical" verse written during the 1930's by such poets as Hugh MacDiarmid, Stephen Spender, C. Day Lewis, and W. H. Auden was more clearly relevant to the era in which it was written because that was a period in which England suffered a crippling depression and Europe witnessed Hitler's rise to power. Sillitoe's dilemma grows out of the nature of his own era, which for him is characterized by complacency, a lack of vitality, and conformity—and out of the inappropriate solution which he has inherited from an older generation of English and Russian radicals—armed revolution. Rather than being a spokesman for common men against the Establishment, the poet becomes the opponent of both. He cannot abide the Establishment because it is in a position of power, and he cannot abide common men because they accept their lot with equanimity:

> King Happiness has waved his magic wand
> Shown you a smooth reflection in the pond
> Of television sets, recorded your own voice
> In self-selections of your choice
> Set up his directions on the street
> Turned mechanic to your motorbikes
> Poured patriot-sauce upon your luncheon-meat
> Sent you out on Sunday-morning hikes:
> Party-hatted happiness is here,
> Each tenet brayed by a loyal chanticleer. (27)

Implicit in this complaint is a longing for a return to a time past which was at once simpler and more demanding, a time when men worked at physically exhausting labor and knew clearly who the enemies were—the bosses, the managers, the owners—when a man did not have to remind his companions of what they should feel. The frustration which Sillitoe faces is no personal eccentricity; rather, it is a common complaint of reformers during the present period. In a collection of essays on contemporary socialism edited for the *New Left Review,* Andrew Hacker observes;

The problem for British socialists . . . is how to produce a political ferment in a society that is generally affluent and most of whose members are content with things pretty much as they are. While it may be argued that there continues to exist a property-less proletariat, regardless of whether its members wear white collars or blue collars, this majority does not feel itself seriously aggrieved by poverty or exploitation or the concentration of economic power in giant institutions. Such citizens will often favor the redistribution of wealth on a piecemeal basis and the gradual introduction of new social legislation; but they simply are not persuaded by the argument that the society in which they live is irrational or unjust or in need of fundamental reconstruction.[2]

The problem is compounded for Sillitoe, for he not only believes in the justness of an equalitarian society but in the necessity of struggle and, ironically, in the positive value of adversity. In his early novels and short stories he looked back upon the difficulties of his youth and young manhood and portrayed their effect upon the formation of his philosophy; in the two novels depicting Frank Dawley, he describes a man who escapes from a secure but boring existence in order to seek adversity and conflict. In a very real sense, the source of Sillitoe's dilemma is, therefore, the prosperity of the age in which he has reached his maturity. The depression world of the 1930's helped to shape for him a philosophy in which the struggle for survival played an important part, but the alteration of economic circumstances in England has made his philosophy partially obsolete, or, at least, in need of revision.

II   *A Falling Out of Love and Other Poems*

A Falling Out of Love and Other Poems appeared in 1964, four years after the publication of *The Rats.* A slim volume, only fifty-six pages in the W. H. Allen edition, the work looks backward to the worst and forward to the best of Sillitoe's poetry. In general, the poems evidence promise, but most of them lack the feeling for cadences, sound, and meaning that characterize the pieces in *Love in the Environs of Voronezh*. Sillitoe treats a variety of subjects: love, revolution, suicide, the moon, stars, desert, atomic holocaust, and death.

Two poems, "Thirteen Lines" and "Poem," illustrate the range of quality and subject matter in the collection. "Thirteen Lines" is another of Sillitoe's revolutionary fantasies. The poet begins by announcing, "I had a vision and must write it down." The vision involves the changing of the guard at Buckingham Palace, soldiers with "Matchstick legs, tomato gut and busby muscatel / Machinely shouldering a gun," and a prediction for the future:

> Tomorrow (when a red dawn comes smoking up the Thames)
> They'll be barracked into sandbag-doors
> And windows, white faces
>
> Firing as the mobs emerge
> Spread through smoking pineapples
> Of blackness at each great gate. (36)

The ungainly rhythms and sounds of "Thirteen Lines" are offset by the skillful cadences of "Poem," a reflective lyric of four rhyming triplets:

> The moon—sunflower of earth
> Held up in darkness
> By each child before birth.
>
> Met by a man only in dreams
> As from a window its face
> Above the meadow seems
>
> Fixed in a memory whose roots recede—
> Down the valleys of the soul return
> To a time before the soul was freed
>
> From that oblivion behind the moon
> That I would follow with my heart
> Though not too closely—nor too soon. (31)

Sillitoe evidences considerable skill here in blending smoothly a variety of metrical forms, most noticeably, the dactyls, iambs, and trochees of the third stanza, and the iambic pentameter and tetrameters of the fourth stanza. The tone and the theme are surprisingly Wordsworthian. As in Wordsworth's "Intimations" ode there is the notion that man possesses true insight before birth, recollects it vaguely in adulthood, and returns to it in death. The reflective and philosophical mood of the poem is an indication of the direction Sillitoe's next collection of poetry would take.

III *Love in the Environs of Voronezh*

While only "Canals" in *Guzman, Go Home* clearly evidenced new development in Sillitoe's technique as a writer of fiction, most of the poems in *Love in the Environs of Voronezh* (published as was *Guzman, Go Home* in 1968) reflect efforts on Sillitoe's part to develop his talent as a poet. The verses are quieter in tone and more reflective in content than those in his earlier volumes of poetry. Whereas in an early poem like "The Rats" Sillitoe seemed to use poetry as a vehicle for expressing the spleen and anger that had not found a way into his fiction, the verses in his latest collection contains few metaphors of violence and are less political in subject matter.

The opening and closing poems provide a key to the change. "First Poem" describes a death by fire, and a regeneration:

> Burned out, burned out.
> Water of rivers hold me
> On a course towards sea.
> Burned out was like a tree
> Cut down and hollowed
> Seasoned by skilful
> Fire into a boat. . . . (9)

The younger, angry poet in Sillitoe seems also to have been "Cut down and hollowed / Seasoned by skilful / Fire into a boat." He has not ceased to attack hypocrisy and injustice, but the focus of his poems centers more upon rebuilding rather than destruction, more upon the quality of inner life than upon external threatening forces.

The last poem, from which the title of the volume is drawn, reflects this change. "Love in the Environs of Voronezh" is concerned with the capital city of a region in south central European Russia which withstood heavy assaults from the Nazis during their 1942 campaign:

> Love in the environs of Voronezh
> It's far away, a handsome town
> But what has it to do with love?
> Guns and bombers smashed it down.

> Yet love rebuilt it street by street
> The dead would hardly know it now
> And those who live forget retreat. (58)

This turning away from invectives of hatred and revenge toward constructive thought typifies the change reflected in Sillitoe's new verse.

A poem illustrating Sillitoe's increased concern with man's inner consciousness is "I tell Myself," in which the persona candidly discusses the "disguise" which he wears to hide himself from himself and from the world. The final stanza concludes:

> If it were possible to shift
> This utterly complete disguise
> I would despise myself
> Through knowing nothing of what lies behind:
> Know all the lies, betrayals and conceits
> That foul up the clear water of the soul
> In order to become one heart and wise,
> And throw away that never utterly complete disguise. (42)

In "Smile" Sillitoe conveys a keen sympathy for the suffering of others. The poem portrays a man who has died, not on the street where a "normal" person would, but in an unused fireplace. What his station in life has been, what caused his death, one cannot determine. He may have been a derelict alcholic or a rich man; he may have died in a mansion or a tenement house by his own hand or by natural causes. What holds the poet's interest is the simple fact of another human being's death:

> If and when, he'd be a normal
> Dead man on the street, and he smiles
> At this mirror that no one can smash,
> Moonless smile of victory
> Insane and constant as the sun
> That cleanses better than the fire
> Or this prison that it once burned in. (36).

A decade earlier Sillitoe in all probability would have made clear that the dead man was an economic underdog and that his death was in some way caused by the upper classes, but the range of his sympathies seems broader now.

Whatever may be said of his past poetic efforts, Sillitoe has come to recognize that the artist at work is essentially a man alone and that, while he works, his decisions should be less influenced by his public self than by his private self. In what is probably the best poem in the volume, "The Poet," Sillitoe reveals a recognition similar to the one which Dylan Thomas voices in his "In My Craft or Sullen Art":

The poet sings his poems on a bridge
A bridge without shelter open to horizontal rain
And the steely nudge of lighting,
Or icy moths of snow that bring slow death
And smother him from sun and moon
Croon him to sleep by snow wings touching his eyes;

Through all this he sings,
No people coming to watch when the snow
Melts and elemental water-forces smash
Between cliff and rock under his swaying bridge.

....

The bridge belongs to him, the only property he owns.
It grows no food, supports no houses
And was so cheap to purchase with the first mediocre poems.

....

He stays young, ignores all promises, requests and prophecies,
But his bridge grows old, the beams eaten and the ropes brittle
And some night alien figures in a half circle at each dim bridgehead
Brandish knives and axes. Lanterns flash,
Blades and points spark like spinning moons
Gathering nearer as he puts away his pens and parchment,
Closes his eyes to sleep, and does not wake up for a week
Knowing that some night he will once more dream
The familiar childhood dream
Of falling forever down the sheer side of the world—
And never wake up. (55)

Clearly, Sillitoe has come a long way poetically during the eight years that separate the publication of *The Rats and Other Poems* from *Love in the Environs of Voronezh*. The strident revolutionary voice of the earlier work has been replaced by a concern for artistry and meaning. Easy polemics have given way to thoughtful reflections on the aspirations and fears that every man knows. And, as the last quoted passage of "The Poet" evidences, the jingled rhymes and galloping meters of "The Rats" have been replaced by a well-cadenced free verse—"free" but disciplined—balanced with alliteration, assonance, and consonance. If Sillitoe continues to write poetry as he has in *Love in the Evirons of Voronezh*, his conviction that he is "a poet more than a writer of prose" may well be transformed from aspiration into fact.

IV *Last Reflections*

What Sillitoe's place in British literature will ultimately be is impossible to say. In several of his novels, in his collections of short stories, and in his most recent volume of poetry, he has made an important contribution to contemporary literature. *Saturday Night and Sunday Morning* remains a unique and an authentic account of working-class culture, and it captures as well the particular sense of rebellion which has characterized the youth of both England and America during the past decade. Arthur Seaton's lack of identification with the relative affluence of his age is, in fact, a criticism of the mass culture which fills the stomach but offers the mind little more than the soporific programs of television. It is a criticism as well of the repetitious, mind-dulling work which is still performed—in the age of the computer—by those on the fringes of society. Perhaps even more important is the determined individuality and sense of self-worth which characterizes Seaton. In an age of increasing emphasis upon conformity in which the conception of "mass-man" predominates, Sillitoe has created a hero who refuses to believe that he is simply the sum of the statistical information which government officials, management, labor organizers, and educationists have compiled concerning him. Arthur's milieu is not simply that of working-class man but of modern man in general—and therein lies the universal appeal of the novel.

Key to the Door contains some of Sillitoe's finest writing. It will undoubtedly remain of value not only as an intensely personal account of the development of a proletarian author as a young man but as an impassioned and realistic portrait of the life of English working-class people during and following the great depression. It is one thing for social historians to record that at that time there were millions of unemployed and hundreds of thousands living on the dole; it is quite another thing to present, as Sillitoe does, the day-to-day existence of one family during that period—to detail the environment of insect-infested tenements, dumping grounds where boys and grown men search for a living, the irrational arguments between husband and wife that arise from the frustrations of poverty, and the demoralizing effect of the dole upon ablebodied men who cannot find work to support their families. In these portrayals Sillitoe has captured the essence of a historical moment that should not be lost to posterity. Sillitoe has also done a masterful job of conveying the gradually awakening sensibilities of a young man born in the slums. The fidelity of his account is testimony to the intimacy of his knowledge of that world and to his skill as a writer.

The last half of *Key to the Door* marks the beginning of a change in emphasis in Sillitoe's novels. In the Malaya sections there is a diminished sense of reality and a growing concern with the political commitment of the hero. The tone is dominated by the author's increased sense of alienation from his country and his preoccupation with armed revolution. These same qualities, of course, characterize *The Death of William Posters* and *A Tree on Fire.*

Style and technique in Sillitoe's fiction are eneven in quality. In general, his best work is his earlier work. The fine rendering of working-class speech in *The Loneliness of the Long-distance Runner* and *Saturday Night and Sunday Morning* is not equaled in *The Death of William Posters* and *A Tree on Fire.* The carefully developed comic situations in which Arthur Seaton was embroiled devolve, in the later novels, into the overdrawn concupiscence and eccentric antics of Albert Handley; the new hero, Frank Dawley, is so intent upon revolution that he apparently lacks the capacity to laugh at himself. Sillitoe's technique in developing suspense and taut dramatic situations is still best illustrated in the stories in the early *The Loneliness of the Long-distance Runner.* The tales in *The Ragman's Daughter* and *Guzman, Go Home,* while competent, generally lack the dramatic intensity and compression which characterize the earlier stories. Mastering the form of the novel has been something of a difficult task for Sillitoe, who is by preference a poet and by instinct a short-story writer. *Saturday Night and Sunday Morning* and *The General* are well unified; and the shifts in chronology and setting in the various chapters of *Key to the Door* evidence careful attention to structure; but *The Death of William Posters* and *A Tree on Fire* are episodic and sprawling. Clearly, Sillitor needs to concentrate on developing structure in any novels which he may write in the future.

If Sillitoe is to fulfill the promise which critics saw in his early novels and short stories, he must return to the esthetic principles operative in those works. Even in the most blatantly anti-British tale in *The Loneliness of the Long-distance Runner,* the title story, we never sense that Sillitoe is creating propaganda and pretending that it is literature. In the stories in that collection, the psychological reality of the characters is always of more consequence than the sociological message which the lives of the characters may suggest. There is also in the early tales an intense drama of man struggling against a timeless and immutable fate—it may be his own character, an indifferent God, or the capricious workings of fortune—but regardless of the particular manifestation of fate, the reader has a sense of being in touch not with this or that political commitment, but with literature that represents accurately and forcefully the human condition. This evocation is the quality which holds the key to Alan Sillitoe's present and future reputation as a fiction writer and poet. If he is capable of returning to it again, his contribution to modern English literature should indeed prove to be worthwhile.

Notes and References

All page references to Sillitoe's works are to the Knopf editions, with the following exceptions: *The Rats and Other Poems*, W. H. Allen; *A Tree on Fire, Guzman, Go Home,* and *Love in the Environs of Voronezh*, Macmillan.

Preface

1. Malcolm Bradbury, "Beneath the Veneer, Pure Animal Life," *New York Times Book Review*, April 10, 1960, p. 5.
2. Anthony West, "On the Inside Looking In," *New Yorker*, XXXV (September 5, 1959), 103.

Chapter One

1. Saul Maloff, "The Eccentricity of Alan Sillitoe," in *Contemporary British Novelists*, ed. Charles Shapiro (Carbondale, Illinois, 1965), p. 95.
2. Alan Sillitoe, letter of May 18, 1967 addressed to the author.
3. F. Lee Benns, *Europe Since 1914* (New York, 1954), p. 284.
4. Alan Sillitoe, "Poor People," *Anarchy*, IV (April, 1964). 125–27.
5. D. H. Lawrence, *Sons and Lovers* (New York, 1958), p. 72.
6. John Rosselli, "A Cry from the Brick Streets," *Reporter*, November 10, 1960, pp. 37–38.
7. Alan Sillitoe, "I Remind Him of Muggleton," *Shenandoah*, XIII (Winter, 1962), 48.
8. Sillitoe, letter of May 18, 1967 addressed to the author.
9. John Braine, *Room at the Top* (New York, 1963), p. 71.
10. Alan Sillitoe, "Novel or Play?" *Twentieth Century*, CLXIX (February, 1961), 209.
11. John Osborne, *Look Back in Anger* (Chicago, 1959), p. 69.
12. John Arden, *Serjeant Musgrave's Dance*, in *The New British Drama*, ed. Henry Popkin (New York, 1964), p. 273.
13. Sillitoe, "Novel or Play?" pp. 209–10.

Chapter Two

1. John Dennis Hurrell, "Alan Sillitoe and the Serious Novel," *Critique,* IV (Fall-Winter, 1960–61), 9.

2. In *The Short Stories of Ernest Hemingway* (New York, 1953), pp. 379–83.

3. Sillitoe, "Novel or Play?" p. 211.

4. See N. Denny, "The Achievement of the Long-distance Runner," *Theoria,* No. 24 (1965), pp. 1–12; G. S. Fraser, *The Modern Writer and His World* (Baltimore, 1964), pp. 179–82; James Gindin, "Alan Sillitoe's Jungle," *Texas Studies in Language and Literature,* IV (Spring, 1962), 35–48; reprinted in Gindin, *Postwar British Fiction* (Berkeley, 1962), pp. 14–33; Hurrell, "Alan Sillitoe and the Serious Novel," pp. 3–16; Frederick R. Karl, *The Contemporary English Novel* (New York, 1962), pp. 281–85; Maloff, "The Eccentricity of Alan Sillitoe," pp. 95–113.

5. Hurrell, "Alan Sillitoe and the Serious Novel," pp. 12–13.

6. Denny, "The Achievement of the Long-distance Runner," p. 10.

7. Sillitoe, "Poor People," p. 124.

8. Denny, "The Achievement of the Long-distance Runner," p. 3.

9. Sir Alexander Paterson, quoted in *Prisons and Borstals,* His Majesty's Stationary Office (London, 1950), p. 60.

10. In an explanatory note in the film script ["Final Screenplay: 'The Loneliness of the Long-Distance Runner,'" unpublished script, Woodfall Film Productions, Ltd. (London, 1961), p. 25], Sillitoe emphasizes the governor's duplicity by observing that Stacey, the best runner in the Borstal before Smith's arrival, will believe in the governor's conception of honesty only "so long as the Governor stands by his rules and principles in even the most subtle aspects. Should the Governor deviate from them in order to give preference to Smith as the better runner when all the time Stacey has believed that it is the spirit that counts with him and not the distance/speed, then there is no further guarantee for Stacey's good behavior." The governor, of course, does just that; he abandons the rules to give preference to performance over spirit.

11. Fraser, *The Modern Writer and His World,* p. 179.

12. Alan Sillitoe, "Both Sides of the Street," in *The Writer's Dilemma* (London, 1961), pp. 70–71.

Chapter Three

1. John Woodcock Graves, "John Peel," in *The Oxford Book of Light Verse,* ed. W. H. Auden (Oxford, 1938), p. 364.

2. Sillitoe, "Poor People," p. 124.

3. Maloff, "The Eccentricity of Alan Sillitoe," pp. 102–3.

Chapter Four

1. Richard Clark Sterne, "Guzman, Go Home and Other Stories," *Saturday Review,* LII (November 22, 1969), 86.

Chapter Five

1. Hurrell, "Alan Sillitoe and the Serious Novel," p. 7.
2. Maloff, "The Eccentricity of Alan Sillitoe," p. 97.
3. *Ibid.,* p. 102.
4. Gindin, *"Alan Sillitoe's Jungle,"* pp. 42–43.
5. Alan Sillitoe, quoted in J. R. Osgerby, "Alan Sillitoe's *Saturday Night and Sunday Morning,"* in *Renaissance and Modern Essays,* ed. G. R. Hibbard (London, 1966), p. 216.
6. Maloff, "The Eccentricity of Alan Sillitoe," pp. 100–101.
7. *Ibid.,* p. 101.
8. Hugh B. Staples, *"Saturday Night and Sunday Morning:* Alan Sillitoe and the White Goddess," *Modern Fiction Studies,* X (Summer, 1964), 175.
9. Karl, *The Contemporary English Novel,* p. 283.
10. Paul Crane, "Binge and Hangover?" *America,* CII (January 9, 1960), 424.
11. Bradbury, "Beneath the Veneer, Pure Animal Life," p. 5.
12. Hurrell, "Alan Sillitoe and the Serious Novel," p. 6.
13. Staples, *"Saturday Night and Sunday Morning:* Alan Sillitoe and the White Goddess," p. 171.

Chapter Six

1. Walter Allen, "The Fable and the Moral," *New Statesman,* LIX (May 21, 1960), 765.
2. Sillitoe, letter of May 18, 1967 addressed to the author.
3. "A Weakness for Music," (anon. rev.), *Times Literary Supplement,* May 20, 1960, p. 317.
4. Max Cosman, "A Rebel of Uncertain Cause," *Commonweal,* LXXIII (February 17, 1961), 535–36; and Gouverneur Paulding, "A War, an Orchestra, a Taut Situation," *New York Herald Tribune Book Review,* XXXVII (January 22, 1961), 29.

Chapter Seven

1. Sillitoe, letter of May 18, 1967 addressed to the author.
2. Frederick P. W. McDowell, "Self and Society: Alan Sillitoe's *Key to the Door," Critique,* VI (Spring, 1963), 116–17.
3. G. H. Bantock, "The Social and Intellectual Background," in *The Modern Age,* ed. Boris Ford (Baltimore, 1964), p. 23.

4. Irving Howe, "In Fear of Thinking," *New Republic,* CXLVI (May 28, 1962), 25–26.

5. Walter Allen, "In the World of the Bottom Dogs," *New York Times Book Review,* March 25, 1962, p. 5.

Chapter Eight

1. Frank Kermode, "Rammel," *New Statesman,* LXIX (May 14, 1965), 765–66.

2. Paul Levine, "Some Middle-Aged Fiction," *Hudson Review,* XVIII (Winter, 1965–66), 591.

3. John W. Aldridge, "Frank Dawley's Dilemma," *New York Times Book Review,* August 29, 1965, p. 26.

Chapter Nine

1. Robert Taubman, "Empty England," *Listener,* LXXVIII (November 9, 1967), 610.

Chapter Ten

1. Alan Sillitoe, letter of May 18, 1967 addressed to the author.

2. Andrew Hacker, "Introduction," *Towards Socialism,* eds. Perry Anderson and Robin Blackburn (New York, 1966), p. viii.

Selected Bibliography

PRIMARY SOURCES

Without Beer or Bread. London: Outposts Publications, 1957.

Saturday Night and Sunday Morning. London: W. H. Allen, 1958; also New York: Alfred A. Knopf, 1959.

The Loneliness of the Long-distance Runner. London: W. H. Allen, 1959; also New York: Alfred A. Knopf, 1960.

The General. London: W. H. Allen, 1960; also New York: Alfred A. Knopf, 1961.

The Rats and Other Poems. London: W. H. Allen, 1960.

"Both Sides of the Street," in *The Writer's Dilemma.* London: Oxford University Press, 1961, 68–75.

Key to the Door. London: W. H. Allen, 1961; also New York: Alfred A. Knopf, 1962.

"Novel or Play?" *Twentieth Century,* CLXIX (February, 1961), 206–11.

"I Remind Him of Muggleton," *Shenandoah,* XIII (Winter, 1962), 47–50.

The Ragman's Daughter. London: W. H. Allen, 1963; also New York: Alfred A. Knopf, 1964.

A Falling Out of Love and Other Poems. London: W. H. Allen, 1964.

"Poor People," *Anarchy,* IV (April, 1964), 124–28.

Road to Volgograd. London: W. H. Allen, 1964; also New York: Alfred A. Knopf, 1964.

The Death of William Posters. London: W. H. Allen, 1965; also New York: Alfred A. Knopf, 1965.

A Tree on Fire. London: Macmillan, 1967; also New York: Doubleday, 1968.

Guzman, Go Home. London: Macmillan, 1968; also New York: Doubleday, 1969.

Love in the Environs of Veronezh. London: Macmillan, 1968; also New York: Doubleday, 1969.

SECONDARY SOURCES

ALDRIDGE, JOHN W. "Frank Dawley's Dilemma," *New York Times Book Review*, August 29, 1965, p. 26. Sees *The Death of William Posters* as reflecting Sillitoe's diminishing creative powers.

ATHERTON, STANLEY S. "Alan Sillitoe's Battleground," *Dalhousie Review*, XLVIII, 324–31. An analysis of Sillitoe's idea of revolution.

BRADBURY, MALCOLM. "Beneath the Veneer, Pure Animal Life," *New York Times Book Review*, April 10, 1960, p. 5. Enthusiastic appraisal of *The Loneliness of the Long-distance Runner*.

DENNY, N. "The Achievement of the Long-distance Runner," *Theoria*, No. 24 (1965), pp. 1–12. Suggests that the cause of Smith's rebellion lies in the failure of contemporary English society to provide a meaningful life for those of the lower economic classes.

GINDIN, JAMES. "Alan Sillitoe's Jungle," *Texas Studies in Language and Literature*, IV (Spring, 1962), 35–48; reprinted in Gindin, *Postwar British Fiction*. Berkeley and Los Angeles: University of California Press. 1962. An analysis of Sillitoe's use of the "jungle" as a metaphor of modern man's environment. Gindin submits, "Nothing really changes Sillitoe's jungle world. A man may win or lose, depending on the wheel of chance, but he cannot control the wheel or change his position."

HURRELL, JOHN DENNIS. "Alan Sillitoe and the Serious Novel," *Critique*, IV (Fall–Winter, 1960–61), 3–16. Contends that Sillitoe does his best work when he does not endeavor to be "serious." For this reason, *Saturday Night and Sunday Morning* is more successful than either *The Loneliness of the Long-distance Runner* or *The General*.

ISAACS, NEIL D. "No Man in His Humour: A Note on Sillitoe," *Studies in Short Fiction*, IV (Summer, 1967), 350–51. An ingenious and perceptive study of the inversion of the traditional theory of humors in "On Saturday Afternoon."

KERMODE, FRANK. "Rammel," *New Statesman*, LXIX (May 14, 1965), 587–94. Discusses the stylistic problems created by violence in *The Death of William Posters*.

LEVINE, PAUL. "Some Middle-Aged Fiction," *Hudson Reveiw*, XVIII (Winter, 1965–66), 587–594. Discusses the theme of alienation in *The Death of William Posters*.

McDOWELL, FREDERICK P. W. "Self and Society: Alan Sillitoe's *Key to the Door*," *Critique*, VI (Spring, 1963), 116–23. An appreciative response to the verisimilitude and symbolism of Sillitoe's third novel.

MALOFF, SAUL. "The Eccentricity of Alan Sillitoe," *Contemporary British Novelists*, Ed. Charles Shapiro. Carbondale and

Edwardsville: Southern Illinois University Press, 1965, pp. 95–113. Sees Sillitoe as a "throwback, an old-fashioned realist" in the tradition of the proletarian novelists of the 1930's and as a natural outgrowth of the "New Left" movement.

OSGERBY, J. R. "Alan Sillitoe's *Saturday Night and Sunday Morning*," *Rennaissance and Modern Essays*, Ed. G. R. Hibbard. London: Routledge and Kegan Paul, 1966, pp. 215–30. Discusses the development of Arthur Seaton and the use of jungle and seasonal motifs in the novel.

PAULDING, GOUVERNEUR. "A War, an Orchestra, a Taut Situation," *New York Herald Tribune Book Review*, XXXVII (January 22, 1961), 29. Discusses *The General* as a confrontation between "the uncommitted pessimist from the complicated West and the trained representative of inhuman tyranny."

PENNER, ALLEN R. "Dantesque Allegory in Sillitoe's *Key to the Door*," *Renascence*, XX (Winter, 1968), 79–85, 103. Discusses Sillitoe's adaptation of Dante's Christian symbols in a novel which is essentially godless and materialistic in its implications.

————. *"The General:* Exceptional Proof of a Critical Rule," *Southern Humanities Review*, IV (Spring, 1970), 135–43. Discusses Sillitoe's reading of man's nature and fate in *The General*.

————. "Human Dignity and Social Anarchy: Alan Sillitoe's 'The Loneliness of the Long-distance Runner,'" *Wisconsin Studies in Contemporary Literature*, X (Spring, 1969), 253–65. Analyzes the conflict between personal dignity and social conformity in "The Loneliness of the Long-distance Runner."

————. "Illusory Deluge: Alan Sillitoe's 'Noah's Ark,'" *College Language Association Journal*, XII (December, 1968), 134–41. Discusses Sillitoe's use of the "jungle" motif and the theme of illusion versus reality.

————. "The Political Prologue and Two Parts of a Trilogy: *The Death of William Posters* and *A Tree on Fire*, A Liturgy for Revolution," *University Review*, XXXV (Autumn, 1968), 11–20. Criticizes the nihilistic philosophy in Sillitoe's later novels.

————. " 'What Are Yo' Looking So Bleddy Black For?': Survival and Bitters in 'On Saturday Afternoon,'" *Studies in Short Fiction*, IV (Summer, 1967), 300–307. Analyzes Sillitoe's use of the theme of illusion versus reality and his technique as a short story writer.

ROSELLI, JOHN. "A Cry from the Brick Streets," *Reporter*, November 10, 1960, pp. 37–42. Biographical sketch and critical commentary on Sillitoe's first three works of fiction.

STAPLES, HUGH B. *Saturday Night and Sunday Morning*: Alan Sillitoe and the White Goddess," *Modern Fiction Studies*, X

(Summer, 1964), 171–81. Ingenious reading of the novel as a reflection of the mythology in Robert Graves's *The White Goddess.* Staples sees Arthur Seaton as the traditional hero-king progressing through "symbolic birth, growth, and death" and "symbolic re-birth and re-dedication to the cyclical ritual."

STEPHANE, NELLY. "Alan Sillitoe," *Europe,* No. 417–18 (1964), pp. 289–93. A general analysis of themes in Sillitoe's works through *The General.*

STERNE, RICHARD CLARK. *"Guzman, Go Home and Other Stories," Saturday Review,* LII (November 22, 1969), 86. Brief discussion of stories in collection.

WEST, ANTHONY. "On the Inside Looking In," *New Yorker,* XXXV (September 5, 1959), 103. Predicts that *Saturday Night and Sunday Morning* will assure Sillitoe a place in the history of the English novel.

Index